Collaborative Observation

Putting
Classroom
Instruction
at the
Center
of School
Reform

Karen H. Peters
Judith K. March

CORWIN PRESS, INC.
A Sage Publications Company
Thousand Oaks, California

For information:

Corwin Press, Inc.
A Sage Publications Company
2455 Teller Road
Thousand Oaks, California 91320
E-mail: order@corwinpress.com

SAGE Publications Ltd.
6 Bonhill Street
London EC2A 4PU
United Kingdom

SAGE Publications India Pvt. Ltd.
M-32 Market
Greater Kailash I
New Delhi 110 048 India

Printed in the United States of America

Library of Congress Cataloging-in-Publication Data

Peters, Karen H.
    Collaborative observation : Putting classroom instruction at the center of school reform / by Karen H. Peters and Judith K. March.
        p. cm.
    Includes bibliographical references and index.
    ISBN 0-8039-6817-5 (cloth : acid-free paper)
    ISBN 0-8039-6818-3 (pbk. : acid-free paper)
    1. Observation (Educational method) 2. Group work in education—United States. 3. Teaching—United States. 4. School management and organization—United States. 5. Educational change—United States. I. March, Judith K. II. Title.
    LB1027.28 .P48 1999
    371.2'00973—dc21   98-40242

This book is printed on acid-free paper.

99 00 01 02 03 04 10 9 8 7 6 5 4 3 2 1

Production Editor: Denise Santoyo
Corwin Editorial Assistant: Julia Parnell
Editorial Assistant: Patricia Zeman
Interior Designer: Janelle LeMaster
Typesetter: Danielle Dillahunt
Indexer: Teri Greenberg
Cover Designer: Michelle Lee

Contents

Preface

Since 1983, the education community has been obsessed with school reform. Millions of dollars and thousands of conference days have been spent in pursuit of so-called breakthrough models, each claiming or promising success.

In our nearly 20 years of experience working with dozens of school reform projects, we have found that the most successful involved substantive changes in classroom instruction. Where successful reforms persist over time, we have found a collaborative method for continuous monitoring and feedback.

Although school reform and collaborative observation are both well represented in the professional libraries of most educators, it struck us that there is no text or manual that *applies collaborative observation to school reform.* The two areas of inquiry seem to coexist without any direct connection, and we felt that a book was long overdue.

We have written this book for two audiences. First, we address school leaders who are working to establish a viable reform program that will improve student performance through the redesign of classroom instruction. Second, we feel that a text such as this is essential for colleges of education that prepare teachers and administrators. Higher education is being challenged by the demand to revamp teacher credentialing and administrator licensure with more relevant and authentic coursework in instructional design and supervision.

Conceptually, the book joins instructional design as the axis of school reform with collaborative observation as the proven method to sustain teacher growth and renewal. We know that acronyms have been overused in the education arena, but we realize that a single connotative tag is needed to expedite discussion. COMPASS was chosen because of its aptness as a metaphor in setting direction and following a course, but it also represents the basic tenets of our system, making it a good acronym. As an acronym, the letters represent Collaborative Observation for Monitoring Practices to Achieve Sustained School reform.

Structurally, the book details a four-part observation process, each component of which is substantiated in the annotated references at the end of each chapter. We have validated the model in our work with more than 2,000 teachers and administrators. All four parts are implemented with user-friendly protocols, and each is accompanied by authentic examples from classroom observations with peer partners. The elements of effective instructional design are incorporated into the protocols and the conferencing processes for the COMPASS model, and they are also the basis for the planning and delivery of quality classroom instruction.

In Chapter 1, we provide an overview of the entire COMPASS model. This includes the rationale for collaborative observation, validation in the extant literature, and corroboration in our own research as graduate faculty and in-district consultants.

In Chapter 2, we discuss the two data collection parts of the COMPASS model: the preobservation conference prior to the classroom visit (Part 1) and the in-class recording of events during the visit (Part 2).

Chapter 3 focuses on the analysis of data collected during the preconference and the in-class observation. We also discuss how to prepare for the postobservation conference (Part 3).

In Chapter 4, we address the collaborative Action Plan as the culmination of the postobservation conference (Part 4).

Chapter 5 is devoted to the logistics necessary to implement the COMPASS model. Included are planning decisions and challenges derived from our work with actual school districts, and particular emphasis is placed on providing the time and opportunity for staff involvement.

We wish to acknowledge the assistance of the following reviewers: Patricia M. Fernandez, Principal, Milton L. Fuller School; Patricia Shoemaker, Assistant Dean, Radford University; Nancy L. Griesham, Associate Principal, Downer's Grove South High School; Libby Hall, Associate Professor, Department of Teacher Education, Preparation, and Special Education, The George Washington University; Martha V. Henderson, Professor and Head, Media-Serials Division, Northwestern University; Barbara Stanford, Coordinator of Secondary Education, University of Arkansas at Little Rock; and Joanne Cooper, Associate Professor, Department of Educational Administration, University of Hawaii at Manoa.

We have enjoyed putting the book together and hope that the COMPASS model will prove as helpful to the reader as it has been to the teachers, administrators, and prospective principals with whom it has been used and through whom it is continuously improved.

Use it well!

Karen and Judy
May 1998

About the Authors

Karen H. Peters is Assistant Director of the Center for Educational Leadership Services and the Ohio Satellite for Effective Schools at Kent State University in Kent, Ohio. The Center provides a variety of consultation, research, and professional development services to school districts. She is also a member of the graduate faculty in the College of Education at Kent State and teaches graduate coursework in educational administration and curriculum and instruction. Her special areas of focus are leadership, clinical and peer supervision, strategic planning and team-based decision making, curriculum development and evaluation, the principalship, and action research.

Dr. Peters completed her PhD in educational administration from Kent State University. She has taught at the elementary and middle school levels in Florida and Ohio, focusing on math and science instruction, and has served as a building principal, curriculum supervisor, and Director of Curriculum and Instruction. She has coauthored a variety of articles in the areas of education reform, staff development, instructional design, the collaborative supervision model, and organization development. With Judith March, she is publishing *Instructional Redesign: Learner-Centered Classroom Reform,* a book to improve teaching and learning.

Judith K. March is Director of the Center for Educational Leadership Services and the Ohio Satellite for Effective Schools at Kent State University in Kent, Ohio. She is also a member of the graduate faculty in the College of Education at Kent State and teaches graduate coursework in educational administration, organization development, and curriculum and instruction. Her special areas of focus are leadership, clinical and peer supervision, strategic planning and team-based decision making, curriculum development and evaluation, and various areas of staff development.

Dr. March completed her PhD in curriculum and instruction from the University of Toledo in Toledo, Ohio, and has completed postdoctoral work in educational administration at Kent State University. She worked as a secondary teacher of English, speech, and drama; as Director of Curriculum and Instruction; and as Assistant Superintendent. She has also worked as Director of Developmental Education at Ashland University.

CORWIN
PRESS

The Corwin Press logo—a raven striding across an open book—represents the happy union of courage and learning. We are a professional-level publisher of books and journals for K–12 educators, and we are committed to creating and providing resources that embody these qualities. Corwin's motto is "Success for All Learners."

Chapter 1

COLLABORATIVE OBSERVATION AS THE CATALYST FOR SCHOOL REFORM

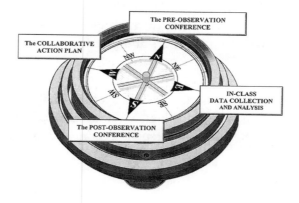

The Distinction Between Successful
and Unsuccessful School Reform

It is difficult, if not impossible, to pick up a professional education journal and not find articles or the entire issue dedicated to the success or failure of school reform efforts. One of the strangest paradoxes is to find one author who sings the praises of Reform Strategy X while another laments its failure. What accounts for the success of a reform effort in one situation and its failure in another? In our combined 40 years of working with school districts and monitoring the literature on school reform, we have seen a pattern emerge that clarifies this quandary. Four features consistently reappear to distinguish successful from unsuccessful school reforms.

1. There are substantive *changes in classroom instruction.*
2. The *initiative is systemic* in that the district infrastructure accommodates its implementation.
3. The *professional development activities are strategically focused* on the reform initiative.

In those situations where the reform was successful, not only at the outset but sustained over time, we have noted a fourth practice:

4. There exists a *collaborative observation process* in which peers assist each other in the ongoing implementation of the new classroom practices and provide feedback about the impact of these practices on students.

Although it is not intended to be evaluative, the collaborative observation process has an obvious impact on the effectiveness of classroom instruction. As such, its connection to evaluation cannot be ignored.

Substantive Changes in Classroom Instruction

Despite the flurry of school reform activity since 1983, many of the recognized leaders in the movement feel that its net impact on student performance has been negligible. Why? Most of the school reform energy has been spent in areas other than the classroom. Changing master schedules, adopting new textbook series, adding technology, moving in and out of "gradedness" and departmentalization, increasing parent involvement, and improving school climate are among the most frequently made adjustments. Although these are certainly worthy improvements, they only tease at the periphery of the teaching-learning process, and once the classroom door is closed, what goes on between teachers and their students is basically business as usual. We are frequently asked by client districts to observe classroom instruction—not obversation of the ubiquitous drop-in variety, but an actual 40- to 50-minute observation. Since 1985, each of us has completed hundreds of observations. In 80% of these classrooms, the only way to know whether it is 1978, 1988, or 1998 is to note the style of the clothing and the haircuts. It is particularly frightening when we work with succeeding generations in the same school—mother-daughter, teacher-pupil. The older of the two report with perfect aplomb how little has actually changed since they were the pupils.

But researchers also acknowledge that in the schools where the focus of reform has been to improve what occurs in classrooms, and where substantive changes have been made in the instructional program, the impact on student achievement has been significant. Those changes in classroom instruction that have been cited in the research as positively correlated with student achievement have been labeled "best practices." Our experience has corroborated these same findings:

1. The identification of specific and measurable benchmarks or learning outcomes for each grade level and content area (the larger point is to achieve a K-12 articulation for greater continuity)

2. The development of year-long curriculum maps that include the sequencing of content topics and process skills, key repetitions of content and process, the appropriation of time frames, the integration of other content areas as appropriate, and the identification of major building events that will affect instruction

3. The development of unit plans that organize the delivery and assessment of instruction as per experiential learning theory and include the following components:

    Objectives, some of which are benchmark achievement outcomes, are taken from the district's adopted curriculum document. These are written at various levels of thinking to include higher-order skills; creative problem solving; scientific reasoning; and the synthesis of various concepts, principles, and ideas.

Motivation strategies draw students into the unit. They reference prior learning, actively involve students, and clarify expectations for the end of the unit.

Information strategies provide students with the information and resources they need to attain the unit objectives. These strategies incorporate various learning styles and modalities; involve constructs such as visual organizers, critical attributes, levels of questioning, and the use of analogy and metaphor; and employ various delivery methods such as demonstration, inquiry, guided discussion, and action research.

Assessment strategies measure individual student mastery of unit objectives. These diagnostic assessments are convergent and involve right and wrong answers to alert teachers and students to any mislearning that has occurred and the need for remediation. They include traditional tests but also nontraditional and performance assessments, all of which are criterion-referenced to the unit objectives.

Culmination strategies also assess student mastery but in a more holistic and inclusive way. Students apply the unit objectives to solve authentic or real-life problems, create or develop a product, construct an object, create and/or perform an original piece, and devise a process. These activities are divergent and can be accomplished through various options; the procedures and products are largely student-determined, and the final outcomes are evaluated using rubrics that correspond to the unit objectives.

Focusing teachers' efforts on the classroom directs the reform energy to the teaching-learning process. But, if classroom reforms are to become systemic, teachers need feedback about the impact of their efforts on students. Traditionally, this feedback is limited to the structured and formalistic evaluation conducted by the building principal. In all but a small fraction of buildings, this is more a ritual or ceremony devoid of any substantive impact on classroom instruction. Every year in our collaborative observation training, we replicate a 1986 survey published by *Learning* magazine that asks teachers to reveal the impact of the principal's evaluation on their classroom practice. Fewer than 10% report that anything of substance comes from those evaluations. We could count on one hand the number of teachers—and principals—

who feel that the exercise results in any meaningful improvements in classroom instruction.

The Systemic Nature of the Initiative

A second feature that distinguishes the successful from the unsuccessful school reform is the degree to which it is accommodated by the district infrastructure and becomes part of the school culture. In our work with districts, those reforms that were adjunct to the daily routines and operation of the system were perceived as temporary and not taken seriously. Unless a reform is endorsed and nurtured by the administration that governs the distribution of resources, teachers remain skeptical that it is truly valued. Without this level of commitment, even the most promising reform soon disintegrates, and practice returns to the status quo.

The need for districtwide commitment is well documented in both research and practice and is best addressed through the following provisions:

1. The district should coordinate its reform initiatives into a focus, rather than pursue a variety of disconnected projects motivated by available dollars. Trying to go in too many directions at one time weakens the impact of each and minimizes the overall effectiveness of the district. The "Plan of Action" outlines a designated role for all staff, and they are held accountable for fulfilling that role. The reforms that are selected should reflect an assessed need and be consistent with a singular and viable Plan of Action that is devised by a team of district stakeholders and that literally drives the total operation of the district.

2. The districtwide reform effort should be focused on the improvement of classroom instruction to increase student achievement. An instructional design process should be selected that includes best practices from the research. There must be an overall design or common set of assumptions for how the targeted reform will look when it is in place; specifically, which

practices will be different as a result of the reform process? Once this has been accomplished, the district must commit the political support and financial resources needed to implement the reform, including professional development, direct facilitation at the building level, and purchase of materials. Job descriptions and performance evaluation criteria must reflect the language of the reform process.

3. If the reform is to actually become an integral part of the district and/or building culture, an important balance must be created between the old and the new. The reform effort will replace practices that are negative, unsuccessful, and ineffective, but it is important to retain those that are positive, successful, and effective. Nothing shatters morale more quickly and creates more powerful resistance than the idea of throwing everything out and starting from scratch. As much as possible, it is critical to retain what works, in conjunction with what is new, to accomplish the reform.

4. If and when a reform initiative is not successful, districts must be brutally honest with themselves as they reflect on the cause of the failure. In many cases, districts fault the reform itself, claiming that it was ineffective. In actuality, it was not that the reform was faulty but that the district either selected the wrong reform for its needs or failed to change the infrastructure to accommodate and sustain the reform.

Districts that are unable or unwilling to commit the necessary support and provide the requisite accommodations to systemize the reforms are better off not to begin. Not only do they squander dollars and opportunity, but they also bring into question their judgment and ability to lead. One illustration of this has been an effort by a state department of education to award individual school buildings monies in excess of $100,000 over 5 years to implement school reform initiatives. Almost exclusively, the control of how the monies were to be spent rested with the planning team of teachers. We found that schools took their staffs to conferences and had great refreshments at meetings with entertaining speakers. But when asked what had changed in classrooms, the response was, almost unanimously, "Nothing." Without the systemic infrastructure in place, very little change occurs.

Professional Development Activities Are Strategically Focused

A third feature that distinguishes successful from unsuccessful reforms is professional development that is strategically focused on the reform initiative. Research and experience alike testify to at least three common professional development pitfalls that lead ultimately to the demise of even the most promising reforms.

1. The reform is merely laid on the staff without appropriate or adequate training.
2. The professional development is limited to an all-at-once crash course that lacks follow-up, reinforcement, and feedback. There is no expectation for staff implementation and no mechanism for replacing old practice with new.
3. The professional development does not require the staff to design and construct their implementation plans and materials in conjunction with their own teaching materials or curriculum documents.

An illustration of the third point above is the strategy used in working with teachers to incorporate technology into their curricula. When we are working with teachers, they will tell us that they went to a technology training program, where they learned about new software but not how to incorporate this new software into their existing curriculum. Therefore, teachers tend not to use the new technology because it is too much work to figure this out on their own. If trainers want teachers to use new technology, they must have teachers bring the curriculum materials to the training and, following the instruction in software use, have teachers blend the two together into their units of instruction.

Improving the way things are done in classrooms and in the principal's office occurs only when staff are involved in designing and delivering the change and are convinced that it will improve the way they do their work. In many cases, the workshop or the materials purchased are mistaken for the reform of teaching practice. In one district, teachers reported that they could no longer teach content area reading because the district did not continue to supply the books. In half a dozen other districts, we have been amazed at the number of teachers who apologize that they are unable to deal with levels of Questioning or Visual Organizers because they were not included in the workshop. Even the most prestigious trainers dealing with the most popular reforms are unable to generate adequate buy-in from staff when the entire program is imposed upon or laminated onto staff practice without suitable integration into the existing culture. Equally unsuccessful are programs that consist of an unstructured series of admonitions that leave a staff feeling either good or guilty, but armed with no different strategies than they had before.

Critical Mass

Another important consideration in designing effective professional development is creating a game plan for capacity building. It is best to begin with a critical mass of staff, followed by the strategic, incremental involvement of the remaining staff within a 2- to 3-year time frame thereafter. With enrollment shifts and staff turnover, protracting the professional development over too many years results in a loss of momentum. Similarly, attempting to involve too many staff simultaneously makes the group too unwieldy to maintain sufficient quality and focus in both the training and implementation.

Both Internal and External Assistance

Reforms work best when districts use a combination of external consultants and internal facilitators. The external consultant provides the background experience and specialized training needed to lead the district through the process. But there must also be at least one internal facilitator, such as a principal, a curriculum director, or the staff development coordinator, to anchor the reform firmly into the district's infrastructure. If the staff do not see one of their significant decision makers directly involved in the reform and following through with directives, materials, and procedures, they will not take the project seriously. Both the external and internal influences are needed for the success of any reform initiative. The external consultant provides the whole-picture perspective, keeping the reform moving in a timely manner and offering the needed technical expertise. The internal facilitator maintains the district's commitment to implement the reform with district personnel and provides feedback to the Board of Education.

In our work with one urban district, the school improvement directors and the data supervisor worked with the teachers' union to implement a reform of the instructional program. During the training sessions, questions asked by teachers were addressed by both internal facilitators and external consultants. This kept the process from being perceived as an external project. There was local ownership, and the district leaders attended every training session and participated equally in the process. In a suburban district, the curriculum director was able to incorporate revisions to the adopted curriculum as part of the collaborative observation process. Teachers then saw a connection among the curriculum reform, the collaborative observation, and the normal operations of the district, causing greater buy-in from the outset of the process.

The Collaborative Observation Process

Although improvement in the delivery of instruction occurs one classroom at a time, and each teacher's growth is measured individually, the *process* by which an individual makes needed changes rarely occurs in isolation. Even if a teacher videotapes him- or herself teaching, most school videotape machines cannot capture both the teacher's activities and the reactions of individual students. And even if this were possible, how objective can an individual be without another pair of eyes? Because every teacher is part of a larger community, he or she is far more likely to take the continuous growth process seriously if it is shared with a partner or two. In our survey of participants about the impact of classroom evaluations, one consistent finding over more than 10 years has been the influence of peers. When asked to identify the most important and reliable source for growth, participants consistently identified fellow teachers.

Throughout the literature, the professional growth model of choice is consistently the peer partnership or the collaborative network model. Its acceptance has become such an icon of both the school reform and the professional growth cultures that *not* to endorse it would be unthinkable. But collaboration and networking are far easier to preach than to practice. In our experience, every district's school reform initiative and professional growth plan include well-worn rhetoric about the value of peer partnerships and the district's commitment thereto. However, very few districts have in place an actual working plan that involves teams of principals and teachers in the collaborative growth process. What we find instead are nonacademic projects that draw staff together socially. Only rarely do we see a mentorship program in place, allowing veterans to coach first-year teachers.

Known by Various Names

The Collaborative Observation for Monitoring Practices to Achieve Sustained School reform (COMPASS) model uses the term *collaborative observation,* but it is also found in the literature as peer review, peer coaching, peer observation, collegial observation, peer collaboration, collaborative peer observation, and peer-to-peer reflection. It is defined as a process whereby teachers observe one another's classrooms to provide feedback on particular aspects of instruction. Specifically, the observer focuses on the teacher's behavior and its impact on students. Prior to and following each observation, partners conference about what is intended to occur and what actually did occur. Most collaborative observation systems do not preclude the principal as a partner, but he or she should be involved as a peer and not from a position of authority. One important distinction we do want to make is between collaborative observation and a peer review model used for contract purposes. The COMPASS model addresses elective, voluntary, nonevaluative assistance among peers. It does *not* refer to the mandatory, high-stakes evaluation process typically known as peer review. This is not to say that the COMPASS model cannot be used to train peer reviewers, but that is the subject of another discussion.

Value or Worth

Collaborative networks or peer partnerships are the cornerstone of professionalization. Through these partnerships, teachers form a community of learners that openly and constructively provides each person with feedback about classroom instruction. The teachers share a common philosophy about the direct connection between teacher behavior and its impact on students. Furthermore, they believe that professional growth occurs from *within* and is not imposed from *without,* despite the authority of the negotiated agreement or principal's role as evaluator. As partners learn to trust each other, there is a greater inclination for each to take growth risks in his or her classroom. Because they share a mutual interest in each other's success, the process is nonthreatening. The strategies that they try are collaboratively devised by themselves and an ally, and they are convinced that the changes will yield positive results. If not, the two of them reconvene to develop additional strategies. There is an atmosphere of encouragement and support for each other as new strategies are attempted to improve the quality of the teaching.

Each teacher has areas of strength and needs for growth and is confident that the partner can be a catalyst for positive change. Visiting others' classrooms on a regular basis decreases the isolation typically felt by many teachers. Collaborative observation implies a shared responsibility among those involved for the professional welfare of the entire group. Talking about instruction from a nonevaluative perspective inspires teachers to think about what they do and how they might do it differently.

We believe that growth cannot be legislated, even with the most stringent mandatory evaluation system. In our experience, weak teachers overtly ignore suggested strategies for improvement as a gesture of control—a show of contempt for a process in which they have failed. Strong teachers listen politely and may even indulge the evaluator to some extent, but they rarely feel compelled to follow direction that is inaccurate. The ultimate beneficiaries of the collaborative process are the students. Not only does the quality of instruction improve in the classroom of each partner, but also the collaborative teacher tends to value learning partnerships and has students work in teams to accomplish various tasks. The entire district must commit to the belief that students learn best in schools where teachers learn as well.

What Makes the Collaborative Process Work?

The collaborative observation process provides an ideal opportunity—and usually the only one—for a teacher to reflect with a colleague on the outcomes of a lesson. By asking appropriately structured questions, the partners enable each other to reflect on their teaching behaviors and how students responded. Partners verbalize and rephrase what happened in a descriptive rather than a prescriptive way, and they make interpretations rather than evaluative judgments. Also included in the reflective dialogue is an indication of how the observed lesson fits with what came before and what will follow. Each partner is able to self-monitor by comparing what actually occurred in the lesson with what was intended.

When the outcomes of the lesson match or exceed the intents, the process enables the partners to identify how specific activities or strategies had such a positive impact on students and how they can be repeated for a similar effect. Sometimes, the observer notes a positive strategy or activity in the lesson that can be used in his or her own classroom.

When there is a discrepancy between the intents and the outcomes, the process provides for the joint analysis of what occurred. In this light, both of the teachers become action researchers as they hypothesize a cause for this discrepancy, propose a corrective course of action, implement specific strategies, and determine the strategies' impact on students. The growth may be dramatic, or it may occur in increments over time. The net effect is that every teacher can grow and become more proficient, and weaker practices can become stronger or be replaced. In one instance where a peer teacher was observing an elementary language arts lesson, the teacher being observed asked students to say how many nouns they heard when she read sentences. Students would respond that they heard a number of nouns, but the teacher really did not know if students understood the concept of noun because they did not have to explain or elaborate when she did this activity. In the postconference, the dialogue was focused on the use of this strategy for teaching nouns and its negative impact on student learning. As a result, appropriate steps were outlined in the Collaborative Action Plan for the teacher to assess student knowledge of nouns. These strategies included the teacher asking students both to distinguish nouns from the other parts of speech and to explain how the same word could be a noun in one context and a verb in another. Through the reflective dialogue, effective practices are reinforced or enhanced and inspire the confidence to broaden one's professional repertoire. The development of an Action Plan for growth is not just for the struggling teacher; Action Plans are developed for teachers at every level of proficiency—the stars, the average teachers, and the strugglers.

Collaborative Observation as
a Monitoring Process

Part of the concern about school reform is that it may not have the desired impact on student performance. Worse yet, even though districts measure student achievement on an annual basis, it may be several years before actual and lasting gains are realized. With a collaborative observation process like the COMPASS model, districts have the means for continuously monitoring the reform initiative while nurturing a culture of collegial growth.

In our experience, we have seen districts make the unfortunate mistake of expecting the building principal to assume the total responsibility for monitoring the reform. For education to be authentically reformed, one of the core values that must be significantly recast is the onus of responsibility for success. The accountability for school outcomes must be shifted from the principal alone to the entire staff. In the collaborative observation process, the principal shares the responsibility for the reform initiative, participates in the training, develops materials, facilitates the peer partnerships, arranges schedules, and procures materials. He or she sets the tone for a collaborative growth culture by participating as a partner rather than an evaluator. One thing we have learned is that principals cannot be forced to exercise this leadership. In our earlier years, we dutifully insisted that principals be persuaded to attend training sessions. In one district, we even went so far as to support their being compensated for their time. As with any attempts to force professionalism—no matter how well intentioned—the results were unpleasant and unproductive. Among the behaviors demonstrated were the following:

1. Some principals arrived late, sat in the back, and remained disengaged (e.g., did not participate in discussions, hovered around the refreshment table, chatted with colleagues about the *real* business of school, etc.).

2. Some did other work during the sessions (e.g., signed papers, opened mail, or made to-do lists).

3. When asked to help teachers develop materials, some principals managed it so that the teachers actually did all of the work.

One of the monitoring functions performed by the principals is to gather and report information about student performance and summarize the results of specific instructional reforms to various stakeholders. A second monitoring function is to determine the level of teacher effectiveness through teacher evaluation. The two tasks certainly complement each other, especially if individual teachers need the principal's intervention. But, because the responsibility for implementation of the reform lies with the classroom teacher, the *major* accountability for monitoring the reform rests there as well. Although the COMPASS model is a collaborative system involving peer partners, it does not exclude the traditional evaluation process. Our experience has shown that teachers who participate in collaborative observation and sincerely follow the Action Plans developed with their partners are better prepared for their evaluations for the following reasons:

1. They are less intimidated by an observer.
2. They are more open and reflective about their practice and its impact on students.
3. They are better able to discriminate effective from ineffective instruction.
4. They tend to be better instructional planners and time managers.
5. They are more accepting of suggestions for growth or enrichment, and they are willing to be accountable for their implementations.

In our judgment, the collaborative observation process is the tool for the continuous monitoring of school reform initiatives. With a shared sense of accountability and responsibility for improving schools, teachers need such a process as they work to incorporate new methods and thinking into their daily instruction. Each of us wants to know how he or she is doing with a new technique, and we all need encouragement to continue trying when our efforts fall short.

The COMPASS Model of Collaborative Observation

The central features of the COMPASS model are the concepts of whole staff accountability and lifelong learning. The model is powered by the idea that adults grow best through a collaborative observation and feedback process. The name COMPASS emerged in part as a metaphor for the purpose of the model. The COMPASS model is a method for locating oneself in what can seem an instructional wilderness, setting direction for successful orienteering, and following the course by watching for various signs of success. The path followed consists of selected school reform initiatives, the ultimate goal of which is to improve student achievement. To avoid becoming lost, wasting time, and/or missing important opportunities, the teacher uses a peer partner much as a hiker would use a compass. In addition, the word COMPASS represents the basic tenets of our system, making it a good acronym for the program.

Drawing together the research on collaborative appraisal, the reform of instructional delivery, and the nationwide campaign to revamp teacher education by the National Commission on Teaching, COMPASS is a four-part process that we have used with nearly 2,000 teachers and administrators since 1987. We have used the program in a variety of settings: urban, suburban, and rural districts, as well as independent or private schools. We have also used the process in a district in Canada. In each of these situations, there was a multiple-year commitment to staff training and implementation of the COMPASS model to sustain reform initiatives. Since its inception, the various elements of the model have been upgraded with input from each group of users, and current research has been incorporated annually.

The process involves teams of teachers and administrators in collegial partnerships who focus on instruction through observation and conferencing. These teams hold Preobservation Conferences; conduct classroom observations; and hold collaborative, reflective Postobservation Conferences, the outcome of which is an Action Plan for growth.

A Structured Program

It cannot be overstated that the COMPASS model is nonevaluative. There are no checklists of required behaviors, and the outcome is contractually nonbinding. However, it is not a series of casual or serendipitous encounters devoid of shape and direction. The model gives just enough structure in the way of format and language to maintain consistency and provide a common set of experiences among participants.

Although we have validated each of the four parts, and the training protocols have worked extremely well, the process is flexible and can accommodate the needs of each district or building. By design, the model is congruent with adult learning theory. At first, conferences and observations are scheduled for the participants because the process involves behaviors and thinking that are unfamiliar. Once the process becomes familiar, participants schedule the conferences and observations themselves with help from facilitators. Training sessions are held at intervals across the school year, providing opportunities to try out the various parts of the model and prepare write-ups to submit at the next training sessions. Because most adults must usually be convinced to learn something new, the motivation for the collaborative observation process is, at first, extrinsic—related to course credit, additional compensation, or a special project. As time goes on, participants experience the success and mutual satisfaction of collegial growth, and the motivation becomes intrinsic and self-sustaining. Consistent with the constructivist learning theories for children, we have found that adults develop greater ownership for the program more quickly when they adjust it to fit their special circumstances. For example, some groups prefer an abbreviated form of the Preobservation Conference, and others have added questions to make it more detailed. Each group decides which materials and notes it will share with the teacher being observed and which should be discarded as rough notes. The program also allows for individual preferences. For example, a classroom diagram is printed on the In-Class Data Collection sheet, but many prefer to draw their own larger diagrams on separate paper.

The Four-Part Process

The COMPASS model of collaborative observation consists of four distinct but carefully integrated processes. In the chapters that follow, each of the four parts will be examined in full.

The Preobservation Conference. The initial process in the COMPASS model is a Preobservation Conference conducted as a structured, face-to-face interview between the observer and the teacher to be observed. The format is a series of questions about the lesson to be observed and the unit from which it is taken. The questions reflect the best practices research dealing with effective planning and include specific inquiries about the delivery and assessment of instruction for the entire unit. Questions about the lesson to be observed focus on what the teacher intends to do and how the students are expected to respond. Having completed the Preobservation Conference, the observer has a sense of how the lesson fits into the larger instructional picture and what to anticipate in the observation. The teacher who is to be observed has the opportunity to verbalize and reflect on what he or she intends to be accomplished, and also to ask the observer for specific feedback about a student or a particular activity.

The In-Class Data Collection. Following the Preobservation Conference, the classroom observation is conducted. Using a structured format, the observer records the major events of the lesson, noting teacher behaviors, student responses, and basic time frames. Space is provided for a classroom diagram to record teacher and student interactions and movement.

The structure of the data collection format also provides for the analysis of what occurred during the lesson. These analysis comments are phrased as a description of the teacher behavior and its impact on students. Having been trained in the best practices research as to what distinguishes effective from ineffective instruction—and, in particular, what relates to the school reform initiative undertaken in the district—the observer applies these criteria to the analysis. The analysis is not done until after the observation, allowing the observer to consider the entire lesson. It is critical to place the analytical comments in proximity to the lesson events to which they refer. The observer is required to recopy his or her notes into a legible script, omitting any editorial remarks or value words. The teacher being observed receives a copy of the script, exclusive of the analysis. The analysis of the Preobservation Conference and the In-Class Data Collection is the prerequisite for planning for the Postobservation Conference.

The Postobservation Conference. Following the in-class observation, the observer and teacher observed hold a postconference to discuss the lesson. To prepare for this conference, the observer completes a form that descriptively reflects the strengths and questions or concerns identified in the analysis. The observer also notes any areas on which the teacher requested observation. Finally, the observer plans an objective for the conference that specifies what should result from the process. In addition, he or she identifies alternative strategies that might be used for a similar type of lesson at another time. The Postobservation Conference form serves as a planning document for the observer and is not shared with the teacher.

The Collaborative Action Plan. The Postobservation Conference concludes with the development of a Collaborative Action Plan. The form includes space for the observer to record the teacher's report of which things went as intended as well as which things did not. When both the observer and the teacher have exchanged perceptions about the lesson, they jointly determine one or more target areas for growth or further professional development. These areas for growth may reflect a single lesson or a larger picture. For each target area, the observer and teacher outline specific strategies or techniques that the teacher will attempt during a prescribed period of time. The partners also identify the anticipated impact on students as the criterion for success. As part of the Action Plan, specific resources for assistance are outlined, and time frames are suggested to guide the follow-up or monitoring process. It is critical to the process that the Action Plan be collaboratively developed by the teacher and the observer during the Postobservation Conference rather than prior to it. Both partners receive copies of the Action Plan.

Insights From the Research

For the reader's convenience, the following citations are organized under headings similar to those used in the chapter.

Substantive Changes in Classroom Instruction

Why School Reform Has Not Been Successful

- Linda Darling-Hammond (1992, 1993, 1995) has continuously worried that teachers lack knowledge not only of the deep structure of their content areas but also of how to select and deploy delivery strategies appropriate to students' developmental levels.

- In reviewing several of the high-profile school improvement initiatives from the first decade of school reform, Michael Fullan (1994) found that teachers had not really altered their teaching and assessment strategies. Even when they strongly favored the changes brought about by the reform, they saw no connection between the reform and what occurs in their classrooms.

- As Executive Director of ASCD during the first decade of the school reform crisis, Gordon Cawelti (1995) compared student achievement data in the 1970s, 1980s, and early 1990s and discovered that there has been little change. Moreover, the reforms made to that point had targeted areas other than the teaching-learning process, and only negligible improvements had been made in classroom instruction.

- In their analysis of the confusion surrounding outcome-based education, Mark Baron and Floyd Boschee (1996) reduced the various excuses for failed school reform to the inability (or the unwillingness) to replace teacher-centered teaching and assessment strategies with student-centered instruction.

- As Executive Director of the National Staff Development Council, Dennis Sparks (1997) applauded higher student performance standards but felt that the majority of districts fail to adopt powerful enough classroom instructional programs to achieve them.

*Classroom Instruction as
the Center of School Reform*

- Barbara Olin Taylor, a legendary proponent of effective schools, and Pamela Bullard (1995) characterized changes in the teaching-learning process as the most profound effect of school reform, where "it's given a face beyond the buzzwords" (p. 41). They advocate turning classroom instruction on its head, shaking it up, saving the good pieces, and tossing out the rest, calling it every teacher's moral imperative to take responsibility for every child's school success.

- In a review commissioned by the U.S. Department of Education's Office of Educational Research Information, Ronald Anderson (1995) discovered that the literal core of each successful school reform project had been classroom instruction.

- In these recent Gallup Polls (Lowell Rose, Stanley Elam, & Alec Gallup, 1995, 1996, 1997), the public included "curriculum and instruction" among its top three priorities for needed school reforms.

- The analysis of school reform in East Austin, Texas, by Richard Murnane and Frank Levy (1996b) contradicted the folk wisdom that the definitive factor in school reform is money. In East Austin, Texas, 16 deficient schools were each given $300,000 per year for 5 years to implement school reform. After the 5 years, only 2 of the schools showed any improvement in test scores. Mr. Murnane and Mr. Levy compared schools to other organizations in that they have vested interests and fixed routines; when given new resources, the path of least resistance is to spend it in ways that change as little as possible. In 14 of the 16 Austin schools, additional teachers were hired to reduce class size, but nothing was done to change what happened in classrooms between the students and teachers. The superintendent was quoted as having said, "You'd go into a classroom—now having only 10 students instead of 30—and see two rows of five students each, working on the same dittos, with the teacher still sitting in the front of the room talking. Things were no different than before!"

- The RAND report on school reform, also presented by Murnane and Levy (1996a), cited disappointing results in student achievement thus far and noted that to substantively increase the performance levels of students requires systemic improvements in the means, methods, and content of daily classroom activity. Unless school reform directly targets the teaching-learning process, little will be accomplished in improving student achievement.

- In summarizing educational reform for OERI, Sam Stringfield and Robert Rossi (1995) insisted that to markedly improve student achievement, we must change what happens in classrooms every day. We need to replace what is currently happening and make it difficult for teachers to go back.

- In the wake of concern about the TIMSS results, a consortium of Illinois school districts replicated the TIMSS test with their own students. When compared with the worldwide results, the Illinois science scores were first in the world at Grade 4 and placed second at Grade 8; their math scores were second in the world at both grades. The researchers (Mark Hawkes & Paul

Kimmelman, 1997) attributed this success to curricular revisions to improve the core academic subjects, the adoption of best practices featured in the school reform and restructuring literature, and increased academic expectations for students.

- After the first 4 years of Kentucky's statewide reform mandate, the National Alliance for Restructuring Education compared the more and less successful schools. Senior Associate Robert Rothman (1997) feels that the distinguishing feature is that the less successful schools began with structural reforms and then dealt with instruction later, whereas the more successful schools tackled instructional reforms at the very outset.

- Patrick Shields and Michael Knapp (1997) summarized several reform projects sponsored by the U.S. Department of Education. In those projects with actual gains in student achievement, the schools had devoted their reform efforts and matching professional development to the redesign of their instructional program. Equally important was that adequate time had been allowed for the changes to affect student performance.

- John Anderson (1997), president of the New American Schools Corporation, reflected on the lessons learned at NAS after 5 years. He noted that even if districts reformed their governance practices and procedures, unless it was accompanied by research-based improvements in teaching and learning, there was no impact on student performance.

- Linda Darling-Hammond and Beverly Falk (1997) were concerned that too often, school failure is attributed to the student rather than the quality of classroom instruction. They regard the teacher as the single most important determiner of student performance, and teaching as the single most important strategy for improving achievement. Genuine accountability, the authors insist, is not so much about measuring student performance as it is improving it by delivering instruction in ways that heighten every child's chances for success. Every student must have access to a rich and challenging curriculum that fosters critical thinking, creative reasoning, and successful problem solving. All students deserve to be taught with methods that are developmentally appropriate and pedagogically sound.

- In response to the nationwide campaign to redesign teacher training and certification requirements, ASCD released *Enhancing Professional Practice: A Framework for Teaching* by Charlotte

Danielson (1996). Included in the four domains are specific behaviors and competencies relative to the planning, delivery, and assessment of instruction. These practices are also prescribed by the National Board of Professional Teaching Standards.

- In reviewing the results of Tennessee's Value-Added Assessment Project, Chris Pipho (1998) reported that the single largest factor affecting the growth of student achievement was the individual classroom teacher. The effects of class size, heterogeneity, and prior achievement paled in comparison to the impact of the classroom teacher.

- Tony Wagner (1998), president of the Institute for Responsive Education at Northeastern University, calls for stepping up reform efforts and invokes the term *reinvention*. He urges all stakeholders to collaboratively decide which academic competencies students are to master and then to identify those forms of best practice most likely to get the desired results. Most important, he insists, teachers must model the collaborative spirit with their students and with each other. The idea is not only to affect academic performance positively but also to nurture students' emotional intelligence.

The Systemic Nature of School Reform

- David Tyack and Larry Cuban (1995), in *Tinkering Toward Utopia,* accused school districts of merely fiddling with reform by taking on legitimate and proven instructional strategies but then nullifying their impact by attempting to wedge them into the culture of the school rather than the reverse. Because they really prefer to hold on to worksheets, rely on the textbook, and continue teacher-centered instruction, districts ruin an otherwise promising strategy. Reform is as much a cultural state of mind as it is political or even pedagogical.

- In revisiting the revolution that inspired the Effective Schools movement of the late 1970s, Barbara Olin Taylor and Pamela Bullard (1995) advocated the gradual but research-guided transformation of a school's shared beliefs. This enables them to envision a new school culture, which, in turn, inspires a new school structure. The process is comprehensive and inclusive, and it holds everyone accountable.

- In a 4-year study commissioned by the U.S. Department of Education to examine school reform initiatives, Ronald Anderson (1995) reported that the success of the instructional reforms were directly attributable to the support of multiple interconnections throughout the district. The relevant processes and documents included board policies and resolutions, job descriptions and performance evaluation criteria, community relations and involvement, the procurement of materials and supplies, disciplinary practices, the system for assessing student performance, reporting of student progress to parents and the community, and the infusion of technology.

- In another such study commissioned by the U.S. Department of Education (Stephen Klein, Elliott Medrich, & Valeria Perez-Ferreiro, 1996), the authors included districtwide leadership that is assertive and proactive about the reform initiative, a shared vision (formulated by all stakeholders) of how things will be once the reform is accomplished, the direct involvement of all staff groups in the reform activity, adequate and continuous staff training specifically connected to the expectations of the reform, and the reorganization of the district infrastructure to accommodate and sustain the reform.

- In his review of 12 highly touted reform projects, respected higher education scholar Seymour Sarason (1990, 1995) concluded that no one aspect of the school operation can be changed without affecting any number of others. In his judgment, systems inherently resist change, and attempting to tinker with one or two aspects without adjusting the others signals the entire system to defend itself against even the most positive change.

- As long-time champions of peer coaching, Bruce Joyce and Beverly Showers (1996) have insisted that, like any reform initiative, peer coaching cannot be successful in a school where the culture is either hostile (negative and untrusting) or apathetic (indifferent and unmotivated). They suggest that building this culture is a systemic issue, and that school leaders may need to reengineer the culture by creating new norms of collegiality, empowerment, and shared accountability for school success. Teachers working in collaborative partnerships to improve the instructional program in each classroom will generate the energy needed to inspire growth throughout each building and across the district. The success of these collaborative instructional efforts will spill over into other systemic features such as parent involvement, physical facilities, school climate, the procurement of materials, student conduct, and co-curricular activities.

- Debra Viadero (1997) reported on the "'Indicators of School Quality,' the National Study of School Evaluation," a broad effort by six regional commissions that accredit public and private schools. The results of the study documented the direct relationship between academic results and system-level practices and procedures. Those schools receiving high ratings had (a) identified subject-matter indicators, (b) frequently determined academic and systemic needs by assembling student performance data and obtaining the input of various stakeholders, (c) designed strategic improvement plans that included student achievement targets and best practices at both the classroom and systemic levels, and (d) documented progress of various systemic initiatives in tandem with student performance.

- Having funded a number of school reform initiatives, the Ball Foundation's G. Carl Ball and Steven Goldman (1997) have indicated their opinion that schools need to adopt a systems perspective in approaching school reform. Schools need to establish incentives for teacher growth, break up structures that reinforce and protect the status quo, install measures of quality control that include frequent monitoring and feedback to staff, and disempower narrow interest groups or subsystems that interfere with the reform effort. In Ballard Goldman's judgment, it will do no good to upgrade the curriculum and adopt improved instructional methods if the administration still permits traditional teaching. The entire school district should organize itself around results rather than intentions.

- The Director of the Peabody Center for Public Policy at Vanderbilt University, James W. Guthrie (1997), identified a huge paradox that has paralyzed school reform. Although they are the most visible and have the greatest amount of power, school boards and superintendents are least positioned to influence classroom instruction. Conversely, teachers are the most directly connected to classroom instruction but are the most protected and least accountable for school outcomes. Reform-minded districts must unfreeze these frames and reapportion decision-making power as well as accountability for student success to make all stakeholders equally responsible for all aspects of the system.

- In an article dealing with standards-based reform, Linda Darling-Hammond and Beverly Falk (1997) expressed their concern that too much of the responsibility for improved achievement has been placed on the student and not enough on the system. Among their recommendations for the systemic support of reform are to (a) establish an optimistic vision that all students will be successful, (b) nurture a culture of continuous improvement in each building, (c) enforce the expectation that teaching methods be aligned with best practices by monitoring classroom instruction, (d) provide various co-instructional services to support intensive learning, and (e) implement assessment practices that evaluate opportunity to learn as well as levels of performance. They also included specific suggestions, such as continuous professional development; reasonable class sizes; innovative scheduling (such as looping, continuous progress, or block scheduling); opportunities for teachers to work together in peer partnerships, team teaching, and other academic settings; and adopting the student advisory system to provide continuous counseling to each child.

- Reflecting on the lessons learned after the first 5 years, John Anderson (1997), president of the New American Schools Corporation, underscored the systemic nature of reform that works. Even the most outstanding instructional reforms cannot exist in isolation. They need the acceptance and confidence of those outside the microsphere of the reform, even if this involves retrofitting school governance to accommodate the reform. Mr. Anderson advocates "focused accountability" and public reporting systems to apply supportive but continual pressure on the school staff to take the reform seriously.

- Former U.S. Commissioner of Education David Seeley (1998) had predicted the current education crisis as far back as 1971. He insists that the greatest threat to public schools is not the voucher system, nor is it any inherent superiority of the independent schools. It is the inability of the public schools to make the deep, systemic changes in their infrastructure that are necessary to support reforms in the teaching-learning process. Their biggest weakness, he argues, is a lack of patience. They try to rush the process, seeking a silver bullet that will spontaneously generate improvements without substantive changes in the way the district operates.

- Thomas Hatch (1998), former director of the ATLAS school reform project, prepared a list of systemic issues that must undergird successful reform. These include technical support for the improved practices in the reform initiative; the reallocation of existing resources and the procurement of additional resources as needed; explaining the reform practices to the local community and keeping them well informed; continuous vigilance for conflict or confusion and the willingness either to resolve them completely or to reach workable compromises; strategic knowledge of how to bring together all of the necessary information, orchestrate the activities, and manage the resources; and the organizational know-how to design, create, and manage reform activities across multiple sites in the same district.

Strategic Professional Development

- As a result of his 4-year OERI-sponsored study of successful school reforms, Ronald Anderson (1995) determined that teachers must be *taught* to make curricular changes and to think differently about the way they deliver classroom instruction. Despite the most optimistic and substantive commitments by a district to improve student performance through the reform of curriculum and instruction, unless teachers are actually retrained and made accountable for changes, the changes that do occur will be only cosmetic and superficial.

- Hayes Mizell (1997), the director of programming for student achievement at the Edna McConnell Clark Foundation, called staff development "a scandal waiting to be uncovered" (p. 5). He claimed that schools have no idea (a) how much they are spending on staff development, (b) how it is determined what to offer (and who should offer it), (c) what purposes staff development should serve, (d) how it is connected to the other initiatives in the district, and (e) how—or even whether—it results in improved teaching and learning.

- Most school reform scholars placed "staff development" at the very top of their agenda, feeling that nothing of substance could occur without it. Michael Fullan (1994, 1996) and Priscilla Wohlstetter (1995) underscored the need for the gradual but carefully integrated involvement of the entire teaching staff in the reform initiative, beginning with a critical mass of teachers and extending to the rest of the faculty in manageable incre-ments. Each author acknowledged that there will always be a few who refuse to cooperate or participate, but those few should not be allowed to derail the process. Both advised working around, over, under, or through them as needed. Fullan (1996), Wohlstetter (1995), and Linda Darling-Hammond (1998; Linda Darling-Hammond & Eileen Sclan, 1992) are convinced that schools cannot be improved until and unless they improve teacher learning.

- According to Judith Renyi (1996, 1998), Executive Director of the Washington, D.C.-based National Foundation for the Im-provement of Education, the ongoing professional development of teachers has "waited patiently for attention while shorter and snappier school reforms have had their day" (Renyi, 1996, p. 37). She insisted that none of the reforms of the past 15 years can bear any fruit unless the nation's 3 million teachers have the opportunity to bring them to life. But teachers are being asked to deliver instruction that is different from what they had been educated to do and in a system that was not designed to accommodate such work. In what Renyi calls the "longest reform," teachers must be provided both the know-how and the time to work on changes, implement new ideas, evaluate the ideas' applicability to their classrooms, and then make needed revisions. Ms. Renyi urges districts to connect the standards of student achievement to teachers' professional practice in com-prehensive school reform initiatives.

- Ted Sizer (in O'Neill, 1995), founder of the Coalition for Successful Schools, said that simply telling teachers who were trained in the 1950s, 1960s, or 1970s to do a better job and then exposing them to a noted speaker at a week's inservice is like expecting a Model T to reach 60 mph because we gave it a new coat of paint or another set of tires. He insisted that "we need to rebuild the engine of the public schools—its classroom in-struction and the skills of the classroom teacher" (p. 4). He joined his contemporaries in the caution against reducing class size, increasing salaries, or adopting any major reform plan without the staff development needed to recreate a vision of the instructional culture of the reformed school.

- In his review of 100 years of school reform, Stanley Pogrow (1996) saw the lack of attention to professional development as missing the entire point of reform. He chides academicians and researchers for engaging the education community in any number of side issues of education reform while artfully dodging professional development as the real concern. Mr. Pogrow acknowledged the importance of self-concept, teacher empowerment, readiness for work, and computer literacy as worthy by-products of improved teaching and learning practices but certainly not the primary focus of school reform. He suggests putting powerful forms of curriculum into the hands of good teachers who are trained to teach even better. Mr. Pogrow wants teachers to be trained in highly specific, systemic, structural methods, supported by high-quality materials that will change what they do in classrooms.

- Stephanie Hirsch (1997), Associate Executive Director of the National Staff Development Council and coauthor with Dennis Sparks of *A New Vision,* advocated a comprehensive approach to staff development that connects all aspects of the system—policy, assessment, curriculum and instruction, and parent-community relations—to student performance and achievement goals. She challenged reform-committed boards to adopt policies to ensure that the district's human and material resources will support only those staff development initiatives that (a) are connected to the district's reform plans relative to student achievement and (b) include accountability for follow-through.

- In their review of the TIMSS results, James Stigler and James Hiebert (1997) focused on the comparison of the educational systems in the competing countries. The biggest problem in U.S. schools, they deduced, is not how we currently teach but that we have no way of getting better. No mechanism is built into the teaching profession that allows it to improve and to continue that improvement over time. Moreover, there seems to be no way of learning from the experiences of successful and effective teachers, no way of harvesting the best ideas of the thousands of teachers who work by themselves to improve their own teaching.

- John F. Jennings (1997), a former staff member of the U.S. Department of Education and now Director of the Center on Educational Policy in Washington, D.C. expressed concern that although academic standards are being raised in 49 states, there is very little evidence that teachers are being provided the assistance they need to help students meet these more rigorous standards. He is convinced that states are telling their teachers to do better without providing the direct assistance they need to do so.

- Judith Renyi (1998) reported the findings of a 2-year study by the National Foundation for the Improvement of Education on the professional development practices of high-achieving school districts. In these districts, teachers assume responsibility for their own professional development based on the needs of their students, professional teaching standards, parent input, and peer review. Peer support and collegial partnerships were the mainstay of the most effective and the longest lasting professional development programs.

- Findings from the study of the first teachers who participated in the NBPTS's National Board certification (Iris Rotberg, Mary Hatwood Futrell, & Joyce Lieberman, 1998) verified the failure of professional development in most school districts. Consisting of 1-day or weeklong workshops, professional development has very little impact on the actual classroom practices in the district. Typically, the sessions deal with classroom management or hot-off-the-press, foolproof programs that are quickly replaced by the next round of workshops. Training rarely deals with the deep structure of classroom practice and the analysis of instruction, and there is not even a pretense of long-term expectation with support or the expectation of follow-through.

The Reform of Teacher Preparation as a Catalyst to Best Practice

- With the emergence of the National Commission on Teaching and America's Future, Linda Darling-Hammond (1996) launched a nationwide campaign to significantly and strategically restructure traditional teacher education to hold candidates accountable for performing best practices, not merely sitting through 4 years of college. The project is endorsed and supported by such heavyweights as the National Council for Accreditation and Teacher Education (NCATE; Art Wise & Jane Liebrand, 1996); the Council of Chief State School Officers (CCSSO; Gordon Ambach, 1996); and the National Board of Professional Teaching

Standards (NBPTS; Mary Buday & James Kelly, 1996). In conjunction with the NBPTS exam, the Association for Supervision and Curriculum Development (ASCD) has published a performance-based teacher training and staff development framework inspired by the Educational Testing Service's 1986 PRAXIS research (Charlotte Danielson, 1996).

- In her challenge to the National Commission on Teaching and America's Future, Linda Darling-Hammond (1996; Linda Darling-Hammond & Beverly Falk, 1997) has called for radical improvements in teacher training and retraining. She calls it "a great national shame" (Darling-Hammond, 1996, p. 194) that roughly one fourth of the newly hired teachers lack the qualifications needed for their jobs. Explaining that no state allows people to style hair, write wills, fix plumbing, or practice medicine without passing an examination and complying with strict licensure and continuing education requirements, Darling-Hammond claims that at least 40 states allow school districts to hire and retain teachers who have not met basic requirements. Her challenge is sobering: "What does it say when states pay more attention to the qualifications of veterinarians who treat America's pets than to those of people who educate its youngsters?" (Darling-Hammond, 1996, p. 195).

- One of the milestone initiatives to identify more rigorous standards for what beginning teachers must know and be able to do is INTASC—the Interstate New Teacher Assessment and Support Consortium (Ann Bradley, 1997c). INTASC has been endowed by the Council of Chief State School Officers, 30 state education departments, the National Education Association (NEA), the American Federation of Teachers (AFT), the National Council for Accreditation of Teacher Education, and the National Board for Professional Teaching Standards. It is also the basis for ASCD's *Enhancing Professional Practice: A Framework for Teaching* by Charlotte Danielson (1996). Also included are content-specific standards for licensure in a few core disciplines and sample portfolio assessments to gauge teacher effectiveness. This three-part licensing system requires demonstrated competence in knowledge of subject matter, teaching-learning theory, and student assessment. Thus, it is congruent with those instructional behaviors identified in the research as best practices.

Collaborative Observation
for Professional Growth

Known by Various Names

- A number of labels have been used interchangeably to refer to collaborative observation or peer assistance. Art Costa and Bena Kallick (1993) suggested "critical friends"; Robert Garmston, Christine Lindner, and Jan Whitaker (1993) referred to "cognitive coaching"; Milbrey McLaughlin and Joan Talbert (1994) described "learning partnerships"; and Bruce Joyce and Beverly Showers (1996) used "peer coaching." Michael Fullan (1993, 1994, 1996) suggested "collaborative teaching" model, and Judith March, Karen Peters, and Heidi Adler (1994) referred to "cooperative learning among adults."

The Value of the Collaborative Process

- In *Improving Schools From Within,* Roland Barth (1990) argued that teachers will grow professionally when they are given opportunities to visit each other's classrooms, collaboratively design curricular and instructional materials, and teach each other. He insists that teachers must first become interdependent before each can be truly successful.
- Carl Glickman (1992) considered peer coaching an opportunity for teacher and peer to *jointly* identify problems with instruction and to *jointly* devise strategies for improvement. Later, Glickman (1993) described peer coaching as one of the most essential tasks in the renewal of America's schools. Through firsthand observation, personal feedback, and reflective consultation, teachers strengthen the overall effectiveness of classroom instruction throughout the district.
- Rockefeller researcher Gene Maeroff (1993) contended that those closest to the work know best how to improve the job, and that teachers are ideally placed to serve as peer researchers. Peer collaboration provides an actual bonding experience, as opposed to merely reading about it or hearing about how valuable it is.

- As two of the seminal proponents of the Community of Learners, Milbrey McLaughlin and Joan Talbert (1994) insisted that when teachers were able to sustain improved practice, they did so through partnerships with colleagues.

- Judith March, Karen Peters, and Heidi Adler (1994) described peer coaching as one of the most nonthreatening methods for connecting the daily instructional program to improved student outcomes. By voluntarily assisting each other to implement classroom practice, providing each other feedback, and making helpful suggestions, teachers take positive control of instructional reform. Teachers are energized and empowered by a healthy diet of companionship, commiseration, and celebration.

- In describing a 3-year cognitive coaching project at a school in Nova Scotia, Wendy Poole (1994) quoted teachers who claim to have learned not only *with* each other during the training but *from* each other during the implementation and evaluation activities.

What Makes the Collaborative Process Work?

- The basis for horizontal supervision or appraisal as set forth by Andrew Gitlin and Karen Price (1992) is a comparison between what the teacher intends to accomplish and the actual outcomes of instruction. At times, there are unintended outcomes that actually enhance the overall quality of the instruction. At other times, the negative discrepancy between what the teacher thought would occur and what did occur requires considerable revamping. Any and all outcomes are discussed by the partners in a nonthreatening, low-risk atmosphere.

- One of the essential features of the Community of Learners, as defined by Milbrey McLaughlin and Joan Talbert (1994), was an atmosphere of trust and safety. Their peer assistance model allows a teacher to grow from his or her mistakes without the penalty of embarrassment or intimidation that surrounds traditional evaluation. It is a low-risk or "hold-harmless" relationship.

- The system of cognitive coaching that is endorsed by Robert Garmston, Christine Lindner, and Jan Whitaker (1993) involves nonjudgmental, reflective dialogue rather than pronouncements of success or failure. Self-analysis is valued equally with the opinion of the observer, and both the teacher and the observer experience growth during the process. Cognitive coaching uses the preconference, observation, and postconference to help teachers improve their instructional effectiveness.

- Carl Glickman (1993) defined the peer relationship as peer in the literal sense, not as master-novice or mentor-mentee, to emphasize the issue of equality. When perceived or actual "position power" is involved in the peer relationship, it takes on an evaluative tone. The entire point of the collaboration between equals is two-way, formative assistance to both partners, and not one-way evaluation.

- The use of videotaped teaching segments and video case studies to promote reflective dialogue is advocated by James Rowley and Patricia Hart (1996). Seeing an unknown teacher on video depersonalizes the process, making it far less threatening to verbalize critical comments. By association, the viewers learn to distinguish effective from ineffective instruction as a function of student response. Seeing oneself on video provides for more direct analysis but is effective only with teachers who are very secure about themselves and are fully cognizant of their shortcomings as well as their strengths.

- Pauline Sahakian and John Stockton (1996) described a collaborative observation process used at Buchanan High School titled "The Teacher-Guided Observation/Curriculum Analysis." Established as a continuously evolving instructional analysis and curricular development program, the process accommodated several of the basic needs of teachers: (a) to be treated as professionals, (b) to grow in a nonthreatening environment, (c) to have the primary responsibility for curriculum analysis, (d) to feel comfortable with change, and (e) to experience camaraderie and consensus. The most intimidating aspect has been to overcome the fear of being observed by a peer. The results have revitalized classroom practice by doing away with the canned lessons that previously had been the mainstay of evaluation.

- Convinced that continuous growth in student achievement can occur only in schools that expect and facilitate continuous growth in teachers' skills, Linda Darling-Hammond (1998) stressed the importance of peer growth programs. In particular, the program should center on the critical activities of teaching and learning, and it should include investigations of practice through case studies, questions, and analysis. It must be built on professional discourse that forces analysis and communication about practices and values in ways that build colleagueship and standards of practice. She regrets that teachers are provided few opportunities to observe and analyze their own teaching and that of others. Earlier, Ms. Darling Hammond and Beverly Falk (Darling-Hammond & Falk, 1997) insisted that districts provide time and training for teachers to provide peer assistance. They applaud New York, California, and Illinois for having included peer assessment in their standards for practice that guide school reform efforts.

Collaborative Observation as Monitoring Process

- In their description of horizontal supervision or appraisal, Andrew Gitlin and Karen Price (1992) described collaborative observation as a means by which teachers were given legitimate voice in what is and is not effective. Without the teacher's perspective, the monitoring process remains *"ahistoric—without context or backdrop"* (p. 65). When teachers determine the intentions of their instruction, they are more responsive to accountability for what actually did occur. What went well and did not go well is more directly attributable to their own behaviors, and suggestions made by those who are in the same boat are far more palatable than those made by someone who is virtually removed from the classroom.

- Jim Nolan, Pam Francis, and Brent Hawkes (1993) suggested that the purposes of supervision were best served when it was conducted more as collaborative action research than traditional evaluation. If the appraisal process is a matter of thoughtful experimentation and pedagogical inquiry, teachers will have a vested interest in the outcome. By contrast, the traditional evaluation system remains external to them, and the checklist of looked-for behaviors is artificial. If done collaboratively, the observer becomes a co-creator of knowledge with the teacher. As reciprocal partners, they both gain from the exchange of feedback, suggestion, and reflection. It is the dissonance between what the teacher intended to occur and what actually did occur that provides the impetus for continued inquiry. The authors suggest the three guiding principles that make collaborative supervision effective: (a) *autonomy* (or teacher self-direction and self-analysis), (b) *evidence* (or observational data of teacher behaviors and student responses), and (c) *continuity* (or the unfolding of the process over time).

- The peer coaching model described by Judith March, Karen Peters, and Heidi Adler (1994) empowers teachers to determine the agenda of appraisal and continuous growth. Based on the principles of Total Quality Management, peer collaboration to improve instruction emphasizes building quality into the teaching-learning process in the first place rather than inspecting errors out of it after the fact. By working in partnerships, teachers commit not just to the ethic of continuous improvement in their instructional delivery but to a sense of responsibility to assist each other in the process.

- Michael Fullan (1992, 1993, 1994, 1996) has consistently advocated peer assistance as integral to the reform process. In his collaborative teaching model, he connects school reform with instructional practice and instructional practice with collegial assistance and accountability.

- Bruce Joyce and Beverly Showers (1996), long-time advocates of peer coaching, cautioned that peer coaching is not an end in itself and is especially not a school reform initiative. It is a catalyst for school improvement, serving to extend and institutionalize the selected school reform practices. They claim that there is no evidence that merely organizing peer teams will positively affect student learning, but in cases where the focus of the collaboration has been the teaching-learning process and its outcomes, the data show measurable gains in student achievement. Once the specific change agenda has been established, peer teams are the optimal way to monitor the reform activity and determine whether (and to what extent) the reforms are having any impact on student performance.

- Paul Caccia (1996) described peer coaching as an excellent catalyst for total staff involvement in instructional discourse. He believes that with its emphasis on sharing, partnerships, open communication, trust, and continuous learning, peer coaching is the model of choice for achieving the goals of education reform.

- The National Foundation for the Improvement of Education conducted a 2-year study on the professional development practices of high-achieving school districts. From data supplied by more than 1,000 teachers and staff developers, Judith Renyi

(1998) reported the dialogues among faculty members as key. Teachers looked at both gaps and overcoverage in their curricular areas and discussed how to strengthen their teaching strategies. They measured the effectiveness of teacher learning through the observation of changed practice.

The "Union" Perspective

- Thomas McGreal (in Ron Brandt, 1996) felt that the teacher unions have opposed peer evaluation systems because they have been designed for that 2% of the staff who are weak and ineffective. He insists that there would be acceptance of a peer evaluation system that served 98% of the membership, one track of which would provide the kinds of assistance needed by teachers who were not successful.

- In a departure from its long-standing objection to peer assistance, the National Education Association has altered its position. President Bob Chase (1998a, 1998b) suggested that each local affiliate place issues of quality classroom instruction front and center at the bargaining table, and these issues should include the formal mentoring of new teachers and peer assistance. He cites the Columbus, Ohio, peer assistance program as a good example. The extent of this commitment was earlier revealed at NEA's annual convention (Ann Bradley, August 6, 1997), when Mr. Chase argued that teachers can provide each other beneficial and reliable assistance, even to the point of counseling them out of the profession if the situation so warrants. Isolating teachers from the evaluation process, he reasoned, was insulting and deprofessionalizing.

- Under the leadership of long-term president Albert Shanker, the American Federation of Teachers has supported peer assistance since 1981. In his description of professional development in the restructured school, Mr. Shanker (1990) endorsed peer assistance as the method of choice for unifying teachers in continuous professional growth. Current president Sandra Feldman (1997) has pledged AFT support for higher academic standards, the implementation of best practices in instructional reform, and specific prevention strategies such as immediate intervention and the abolition of social promotion. Ms. Feldman insisted that teachers must have the time and opportunity to work in partnerships and collaborative teams to strengthen the overall quality of instruction in each building. She points proudly to peer assistance programs in Cincinnati and Toledo, Ohio; Rochester, New York; Pittsburgh, Pennsylvania; and Poway, California.

Chapter 2

COLLECTING DATA:
PRIOR TO AND DURING
CLASSROOM OBSERVATION

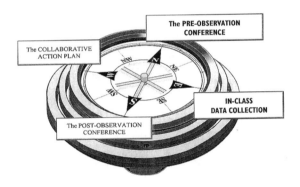

For the COMPASS model to be successful, descriptive and nonjudgmental information must be gathered prior to and during the classroom observation. Both the observer and the teacher to be observed must be skilled at conferencing techniques, describing instruction, and recording information. In contrast to traditional evaluation, which is hierarchical because the teacher being observed is subordinate to the observer, collaborative observation is a partnership in which both partners share equally the responsibility for the outcome. As such, each must alternately play both the role of the teacher observed and the observer.

The Preobservation Conference

The Preobservation Conference serves three important purposes. First, rapport and trust are established through a dialogue about instruction. Second, the observer becomes familiar with the lesson and understands what the teacher intends to accomplish. In a larger context, he or she sees how this lesson fits into the total unit or framework. Third, the teacher is provided a rare opportunity to talk about what he or she does in planning instruction, and the mental run-through of the lesson is like a reflection in advance. It bears repeating that the preobservation conference is a face-to-face interview between the observer and teacher. The observer records the teacher's responses as he or she talks through each question. It is strongly suggested that the teacher see the form in advance, but it should be made clear that he or she should not complete the form. It is the dialogue during the Preobservation Conference that helps build the rapport and trust of a peer partnership. At the conclusion of the Preobservation Conference, both partners have made an investment in the lesson and have a stake in its success.

Figure 2.1 represents the protocol for the Preobservation Conference.

The Preobservation Conference in the COMPASS model is a departure from others that we have seen. In our experience as school reform consultants, we continuously review the research on instructional design and the improvement of the teaching-learning process. The questions we have included in the Preobservation Conference reflect the best practices advocated in the school reform literature. We have found that if the school district's reform initiative includes such practices, and if the teachers have been trained properly, then these questions validate their training and reinforce the district's expectation that such practices will be used in the classroom. In cases where participants were not trained in best practices before their involvement in the COMPASS model, they became aware of them through the collaborative observation process. In one extremely affluent district, the expectation was established by the administrative team that each unit of instruction must include at least one performance assessment accompanied by a scoring rubric that paralleled the unit objectives. During the Preobservation Conference in this district, one of the questions dealt with performance assessments and rubrics. Several districts require teachers to provide intervention for students who fail

---

The COMPASS Model of Collaborative Observation
Pre-Observation Conference: Part I

Observer:_____   Observation Number: _____

Teacher Observed:_____   Conference Date/Time:_____

Subject:_____ Grade Level: _____   Observation Date/Time: _____

UNIT

1. What is the title of the **UNIT**/chapter?   2. How much time do you spend on this **UNIT**?

_____   _____

3. What are the objectives for this **UNIT**? The students will . . .

1. _____

2. _____

3. _____

4. _____

5. _____

4. How are these objectives related to content and objectives in other subject areas?

_____

_____

5. **MOTIVATION**: How will/did you <u>introduce</u> or <u>motivate</u> students for the **UNIT**?

6. **INFORMATION**: What <u>content/concepts</u> are taught and with what <u>methods</u> for the **UNIT**?

7. **ASSESSMENT**: How will you <u>assess</u> what students have learned in the **UNIT**?

8. **CULMINATION**: How will students <u>integrate</u> what they have learned in the **UNIT**?

Figure 2.1. Preobservation Conference: Part 1

to master unit objectives. These districts include a question on the Preobservation Conference asking what the teacher has planned for intervention.

The format for the Preobservation Conference features two main elements: the unit plan, or overall framework, and the lesson to be observed. Questions 1 through 8 relate to the unit or larger picture; this is often referred to as the theme, chapter, or section. Hereafter, for the sake of convenience, we refer to this as the unit. In traditional evaluation (and even in the most celebrated collaborative supervision models), the emphasis is on the lesson to be observed without regard for the larger context. This narrow focus creates a silo effect; teachers need only concern themselves with making one or two lessons exemplary. In our experience, if teachers become accustomed to thinking about the broader context of their planning, their overall planning will improve. The focus shifts from staging one or two model lessons exclusive of the rest of the year to a broader context or more inclusive view of planning.

Preobservation Conference Form:
Questions 1–8: The Unit Plan

Title and time frame. The teacher is asked to identify the title of the unit and the amount of time spent on it relative to the entire year. This reinforces the importance of connections between and among pieces of content. In those cases where teachers are working on content for an entire year or semester (e.g., estimation or word attack skills), the observer presses for how this particular application of the content differs from what happens at other points during the year. One best practice is to contextualize repeated content within a variety of activities. The word attack skills example should reappear with subsequent literature selections, writing assignments, and/or readings from various other content areas. Estimation should occur as part of measurement, geometry, data analysis, and so on.

Unit objectives. Although teachers are accustomed to identifying the objectives for a single lesson, we feel that it is essential to reference the objectives for the entire unit. Standards-based reform calls for districts to identify achievement benchmarks or learning outcomes for each subject area. Although most districts have courses of study or curriculum documents, it has been our experience that many teachers do not reference them in their planning. It is these teachers who are unable to articulate what is expected of the students by the end of the unit. Instead, they list activities or their own behaviors. They also tend to offer objectives that are poorly phrased, such as "understand," "explore," "learn," or "appreciate." Once teachers have worked in a standards-based reform project, they become proficient at identifying effective unit objectives as per the best practices criteria. Objectives that are written effectively do the following:

1. Allude to the curriculum document for the district and include one or more major achievement benchmarks
2. Are expressed as verb phrases of the student's performance—not the teacher's behavior
3. Are tied to previous and subsequent learning
4. Require students to use a variety of levels of thinking
5. Are congruent with the delivery and assessment techniques
6. Represent mental constructs that students use to internalize content and demonstrate mastery

Because the observer is equally proficient with these criteria, he or she is able to delve or probe in an affirming way to help the teacher clarify appropriate objectives.

Integration with other subjects. One of the most frequently endorsed best practices is to provide students with multiple contexts for learning wherever possible. Because life experiences are not compartmentalized into math, language, science, and so forth, the skills and knowledge that students need to solve problems and think critically and creatively should not be taught in isolation. As such, teachers are asked how the connections are made between and across subject areas.

The next four questions on the Preobservation Conference form reflect the best practices research and tie conceptually into experiential learning theory. The answers to these questions tell the observer how the teacher has planned to deliver and assess the unit objectives according to the criteria for best practices. They also provide the teacher with an opportunity to verbalize and clarify the decisions he or she has made about the instructional process. If the observer does not hear the criteria within the teacher's response, he or she seeks further clarification with probing questions. The observer must distinguish the difference between delving for additional information and making the teacher feel as if his or her answer is incorrect. If a couple of probes do not yield additional information, the observer should move on. The issue is often clarified later in the conference.

Motivation. The motivational activities for each unit are expressly designed to draw students into the unit. These activities serve as hooks or anchors for subsequent reference, especially when students encounter difficult material or lose focus. The observer asks questions about the motivation and listens for the following criteria to be reflected in the teacher's responses:

1. Students are actively engaged to provide a direct, concrete connection to the unit.
2. Activities connect the unit objectives to prior and subsequent learning.
3. Activities are constructed to disclose what students already know or do not know about the unit.
4. The end-of-unit expectations are made clear in terms of what students will be required to produce, construct, or perform.

Information. The information activities are those through which students construct the knowledge they will need to master the unit objectives. The teacher will address the knowledge, concepts, ideas, and/or processes to be taught and will specify the delivery strategies that are congruent with the demands of the objectives. The questions asked by the observer are structured so that the teacher includes the following criteria in his or her responses:

1. All unit objectives are taught using methods that are congruent with intended outcomes.
2. Activities outlined imply the teacher's behavior and indicate how students are to respond.
3. Students are actively engaged in a variety of delivery strategies to construct new knowledge.
4. Activities involve one or more sensory channels.
5. The amount of time that students spend receiving information is balanced with the time they spend using information in practice and independent situations.

Assessment. Although effective teachers monitor student progress throughout the unit, making corrections and adjustments as needed, a more formal measure of learning occurs at the conclusion of the information activities. Whether traditional paper-and-pencil tests or nontraditional assessments, these measures are criterion-referenced to the unit objectives. The teacher's response to this question tells the observer whether the assessment activities:

1. Are congruent with the intent and scope of the unit objectives and aligned with the information strategies
2. Are diagnostic to help identify areas of strength and those in need of reteaching
3. Require students to think at different levels
4. Focus on individual student mastery of the outcomes

Culmination. The final question about the unit plan relates to how students demonstrate ownership of their new learning. These culminating activities are also an assessment but at a more divergent, holistic, and summative level than the diagnostic measures in the previous section. These assessments draw the unit objectives together, requiring students to complete an authentic or real-world project to demonstrate independent mastery. The observer listens for the teacher to describe activities that do the following:

1. Draw together all that has occurred in the unit
2. Focus on authentic or real-world projects
3. Integrate with other content areas as appropriate
4. Are divergent to allow for student input and choice
5. Use a rubric or checklist to evaluate the performance

The collaborative observation may be taking place in the middle or near the end of the unit. In these cases, many of the responses given by the teacher during the Preobservation Conference will be referenced in the past tense rather than as what the teacher plans to do. Over the years, we have discovered that these questions about the unit actually become expectations within the COMPASS partnerships and thus are integrated into the planning routines of every participant to make best practices an integral part of the instructional delivery system in a building.

Preobservation Conference Form:
Questions 9-12: The Daily Lesson Plan

Once the observer has a sense of the unit as a larger context for the lesson to be observed, it is important for him or her to zero in on the lesson itself. As shown in Figure 2.2, the second page of the Preobservation Conference protocol contains the following questions.

The COMPASS Model
Pre-Observation Conference: Part II

LESSON

9. Where does this **lesson** occur in the Unit? ___Motivation ___Information ___Assessment ___Culmination

10. Which **OBJECTIVE(S)** are involved in the **lesson**? _____

11. Outline the **LESSON** I will see -- give time frames, what you will do, what students will do, and the type of grouping arrangement. [Be sure that teacher tells you specific content to be dealt with in the lesson.]

Time	What will you do?	What will students do?	Grouping/Physical Setting # of Students _____

12. What specific areas of the **LESSON** do you want me to observe?

Figure 2.2. Preobservation Conference: Part 2

Questions 9 and 10. The observer asks the teacher where in the unit this lesson falls and which of the unit objectives will be addressed. The answers to these questions indicate the extent to which the teacher has appropriately structured the lesson according to its relative position in the unit. By identifying the specific objectives involved in the lesson, the teacher demonstrates knowledge about the developmental sequence of learning outcomes.

Question 11. The intent of this question is for the observer to hear the teacher talk through the major events of the lesson. The response should include approximate time frames, teaching strategies—specifying both the content and technique—and the intended student responses or behaviors. One of the most highly valued aspects of the COMPASS model is that it frames classroom instruction in two dimensions: teacher behavior—or what the teacher intends to do—and student response—or how the teacher intends for the student to respond. The key in the analysis that follows the In-Class Data Collection is the determination of the direct relationship between the two. If not indicated by the teacher, the observer will ask him or her to describe the physical setting of the classroom and explain how children will be grouped during the lesson.

Question 12. One of the most important functions of the Preobservation Conference is to maximize teacher ownership of the process by allowing him or her to determine a major area of focus to be observed during the lesson. Usually, teachers answer this question with the names of students; a particular strategy or technique being attempted; or an area of need, such as moving students in and out of groups.

Although the Preobservation Conference protocol delineates 12 separate questions, our experience has been that one prompt generally yields the response to several questions without having to ask each one separately.

The key to a successful Preobservation Conference is that it be a natural conversation about teaching. The observer and the teacher observed must have a discussion rather than simply ask and answer questions.

Preobservation Conference Summary

Consistent with the research on instructional reform, the quality of classroom practice is directly attributable to the effectiveness of planning. Throughout the Preobservation Conference, the observer has been listening for answers about the teacher's planning. If the teacher's responses to the Preobservation Conference reflect the criteria listed for each section, it is more likely that the actual delivery will be consistent with those best practices that are the targets of the reform initiative. If followed through, these reform practices are distinct from traditional planning and delivery in at least four major ways:

1. There will be congruence among the intended outcomes or objectives, the teaching methods, and the assessment techniques.
2. The classroom activities will be student centered rather than teacher focused.
3. The students actually construct their own knowledge rather than repeat or mimic the teacher's.
4. Learning and assessment activities will be authentic in that they simulate real-life experiences or performances that require students to apply the unit objectives.

Because participants in the process play the role of both teacher and observer, the exchange is mutually beneficial and completely nonthreatening. Our experience has been that once participants own the process, the teacher asks the observer for feedback and suggestions during the conference itself. This takes the Preobservation Conference to an even higher level of collaboration, increasing the observer's investment in the success of the lesson and enhancing the level of trust between the partners. It is important to note that no matter how many times we stress to participants that the Preobservation Conference is a face-to-face exchange about the unit and the lesson, someone invariably places the form in the teacher's mailbox. During our debriefings, the participant actually expresses surprise that the teacher was upset.

The research has shown that the usefulness and reliability of the data collected during the observation are directly related to the amount and type of information that the teacher has considered and given to the observer prior to the observation.

Figure 2.3 illustrates a completed Preobservation Conference protocol for a fifth-grade World Studies lesson. This same lesson will be used to illustrate each of the other parts of the process.

The In-Class Data Collection Process

There should be no more than a day or two between the Preobservation Conference and the in-class observation. The COMPASS model uses a modified scripting format to capture lesson events during the classroom observation. Whereas other models use formats that address "close-up" targets (e.g., tallies for the number of times something occurs,

---

The COMPASS Model of Collaborative Observation
Pre-Observation Conference

Observer: *Sample*   Observation Number: *2*

Teacher Observed: *Dan*   Conference Date/Time: *10/15 11:25*

Subject: *World Studies*   Grade Level: *5*   Observation Date/Time: *10/17 8:05*

UNIT

1. What is the title of the UNIT/chapter?

    The Spanish Conquest of Mexico

2. How much time do you spend on this UNIT?

    2 weeks

3. What are the objectives for this UNIT? The students will . . .

    1. *describe cultural aspects of Aztec life*

    2. *compare Aztec culture to our own*

    3. *explain how the Spanish conquered Mexico and their treatment of the Aztecs*

    4. *analyze the political correctness of one culture attempting to impose its beliefs on another*

    5. *relate the conquering of the Aztecs to current global events*

4. How are these objectives related to content and objectives in other subject areas?

    Art: sculpture, paintings; Language Arts: vocabulary, word origins, related literature;

    Math: engineering, construction

5. **MOTIVATION:** How will/did you introduce or motivate students for the UNIT?
    *   *students read introduction to the chapter*
    *   *class discussion about Mexico to see what they already knew before starting*
    *   *showed slides and pictures of Mexico*
    *   *explained the final project -- play or debate*

6. **INFORMATION:** What content/concepts are taught and with what methods for the UNIT?
    *   *aspects of Aztec life prior to Spanish arrival: lecture; slides (religion, culture, economics, etc.)*
    *   *events of the Conquest: lecture; filmstrip*
    *   *relate to current or similar world situation: lecture; newspapers; magazines; Internet*
    *   *compare Aztec culture to students' own culture: filmstrips; pictures/posters; lecture; class discussion*
    *   *relate this conquest to more modern-day circumstances*

7. **ASSESSMENT:** How will you assess what students have learned in the UNIT?
    *   *paper-pencil test (including an essay analyzing a recent or similar world situation in relationship to the Aztec situation; scored using rubric)*
    *   *study guides*
    *   *participation in guided discussions*

8. **CULMINATION:** How will students integrate what they have learned in the UNIT?
    *   *role-play (debate) between the Aztecs and the Spaniards to evaluate the ethics involved in one culture overtaking another*

Figure 2.3. Preobservation Conference   *(continued)*

The COMPASS Model

LESSON

9. Where does this lesson occur in the Unit? ___Motivation ___Information ___Assessment ✓ Culmination

10. Which **OBJECTIVE(S)** are involved in the lesson? *review of #1-5; focus on 4*

11. Outline the LESSON I will see -- give time frames, what you will do, what students will do, and the type of grouping arrangement. [Be sure that teacher tells you specific content to be dealt with in the lesson.]

Time	What will you do?	What will students do?	Grouping/Physical Setting # of Students _22_
5 minutes	relate Spanish conquest of Aztecs to student life (review)	answer questions	whole group; desks in rows
15 minutes	review Aztecs—describe the setting, their cities, the religion, and the pyramids, also school (relate to current times)	answer questions	
15-20 minutes	set up for, and conduct role-play of Aztecs and Spanish	students take the role of an Aztec or Spaniard debate various situations given by the teacher	students in various roles: half Aztecs/half Spanish

12. What specific areas of the **LESSON** do you want me to observe?

how well the debate goes

Figure 2.3. *Continued*

or documentation of interpersonal communications), the script format is better suited to the wide-angle snapshot required of most collaborative appraisals (see Figure 2.4). The observer needs to capture enough detail to reconstruct the major lesson events for the Postobservation Conference but does not need to do a verbatim script unless requested by the teacher. Note the lesson analysis headings on the script

The COMPASS Model

IN-CLASS DATA COLLECTION

Classroom Drawing	

Observer:_____

Teacher Observed:_____

Materials:_____

_____

_____

Date:_____   Number of Students:_____

	Lesson Description		Lesson Analysis	
Time	Teacher Behavior	Student Behaviors/Responses	Strengths	Concerns/Questions

Figure 2.4. Blank Script Page   *(continued)*

form to the right of the student response columns. These lesson analysis columns will not be used until after the observation is completed.

In-Class Data Collection Format

The classroom diagram. As part of the script form, the classroom diagram is useful for several purposes. It shows the placement of bookshelves, student desks, teacher movements, the teacher's desk, materials and equipment, and other important physical features. During the observation itself, this diagram provides a field for recording the movements of the teacher and students and for noting the verbal exchanges among students and between the students and teacher. By indicating a description of each student and the number of times he or she asks or answers a question, the observer can help the teacher recap which students were more and less actively involved during the lesson.

Observer: _____			Page: _____	
Lesson Description			**Lesson Analysis**	
Time	**Teacher Behavior**	**Student Behaviors/Responses**	**Strengths**	**Concerns/Questions**

Figure 2.4. *Continued*

Script of lesson events. The two most important pieces of information to be recorded during the lesson are the teacher behaviors and the student responses. At the outset, participants usually attempt to record too much detail and miss most of what is happening. Naturally, they complain and ask why they must script. Because we realize that they will change their perceptions about this, we hold firm. As the year progresses, participants become proficient at scripting key events and interactions without missing the lesson. They discover that scripting literally includes them as participants in the lesson and not merely as spectators. Early on, it is helpful to novice scripters to be given a few tips:

1. Capture a brief description of each teacher behavior (e.g., "Civil War—question and answer" or "three states of matter—group discussion").

2. Capture the essence of the student's response, rather than merely writing "answered question." It is important to include a key word or two as an indication of whether the answer given was correct or incorrect.

3. Capture whether the teacher acknowledged the student's response as correct or incorrect and what feedback was given.

4. Clock the time that the activity shifted; this allows a teacher to compare how long an activity took with how long he or she planned for it to take and how much time was used in transition.

5. Avoid the use of any prescriptive words or qualifiers, such as "good," "excellent," "poor," or "weak." The script detail is to be descriptive of the lesson events.

Observers must devise a shorthand code of their own to capture the lesson events. They must then condense several sheets of "scratchings" that may be unintelligible into two or three neatly lettered pages to share with the teacher. This permits the observer to reexperience the lesson as he or she rewrites the script to review with the teacher. In essence, the observer and the teacher must be able to use the script and the classroom diagram to reconstruct the lesson in terms of what the teacher did and how students responded.

Refinements to the
In-Class Data Collection

Once participants become proficient in scripting, they have learned that "enough detail" is further determined by the teacher's response to Item 12 of the Preobservation Conference. For example, the teacher may have asked the observer to note the level of questions asked or the way directions were given. This may necessitate near-verbatim scripting. For more impressionistic reactions, key words might suffice.

Although skeptical in the beginning, both partners realize the importance of the script as the *definitive* document for the Postobservation Conference. Without it, reflective dialogue about the teacher's behaviors and their impact on students is limited to memory.

Figure 2.5 represents a portion of the script that would be recorded for the fifth-grade World Studies observation detailed in the Preobservation Conference.

The COMPASS Model	IN-CLASS DATA COLLECTION

Classroom Drawing

Map

Teacher Desk *Teacher*   *Table*
(*books, fliers*)

2 absent

Linda	*Trevor*	*Susie*	*Beth*	*Troy*
Pete✓	*Bert*	*Bob*	*Max*	*Steven✓*
Sonja✓	*Lori*	*Chris(male)✓ ✓ X*		*Heather*
Bill	*John✓ ✓*	*Iris*	*Will*	*Sam*
Jim	*Lucy*		*Melissa*	*Danielle*
X				

Observer: ___*Sample*___

Teacher Observed: ___*Dan*___

Materials: ___*supplemental texts, notebooks, notecards*___

Date: ___*10/17*___   Number of Students: ___*23*___

	Lesson Description		Lesson Analysis	
Time	**Teacher Behavior**	**Student Behaviors/Responses**	**Strengths**	**Concerns/Questions**
8:05	*Aztecs . . . American Indian Race reviewed words from Nahuatl that are still used today*			

	City Life
	   City name - Tan . . .
	   Build on Lake _____
		[students give correct response as a group]		

	How many people did Cortez have? *Close. 600*	*Chris: 500!*		

	Religion
	   Prisoners
	   Sacrifice
	   Spelled name of god (I could not get it down)
	   volcanic/knife			

Figure 2.5. Sample Script   *(continued)*

Summary

The data collection portion of the COMPASS model consists of the Preobservation Conference and In-Class Data Collection. The protocols for each are detailed, but collectively, their components represent a comprehensive synopsis of best practices from the research on instructional reform.

Throughout the years, participants consistently ask whether the protocols should be shared with the teacher observed. Because the entire process is collaborative, the answer is yes, but with a few cautionary notes. The Preobservation Conference is constructed to be

Observer:_____   Page:___2___

	Lesson Description		Lesson Analysis	
Time	Teacher Behavior	Student Behaviors/Responses	Strengths	Concerns/Questions
	What if they sacrificed and they still had eclipse?	*Chris: they didn't sacrifice enough*		
	plumed serpent . . . *Why did Montezuma fear him?* *What else?* *Was he driving a Chevrolet?*	*Pete: Quetacquala (sp)* *fair skinned* *[laughter!!]* *riding a horse (several say)*		
	Montezuma made big mistake *Cortez figured there was more*	*[students as group] gave him the gold*		
8:13	*[showed article from magazine with Aztecs. Held up pictures for class to see.]*			
	Pyramids *What is outstanding about their pyramids?*	*John: they had no machines to move the rocks*		
	How big? *20 stories*			
	Any questions?			

Figure 2.5. *Continued*   *(continued)*

a face-to-face interview and should, under no circumstances, be given to the teacher to complete prior to the conference. The entire COMPASS model is driven by face-to-face exchanges, and to circumvent the process of recording a teacher's responses as he or she gives them eliminates the rapport and affirmation that result from genuine interest and active listening. It is recommended that a blank copy of the Preobservation Conference form be available to the teacher being observed to enable him or her to consider his or her responses in advance. The teacher should also be provided with a copy of the script but only after it has been recopied; this will eliminate extraneous detail, value words, and illegible writing.

Observer:			Page: _3_	

Lesson Description			Lesson Analysis	
Time	Teacher Behavior	Student Behaviors/Responses	Strengths	Concerns/Questions
	They had schools outstanding students became priests; average students were in houses of youth. Most of us are average, a few would be priests.			
8:20	*Now, something interesting. We will find out who is right and who is wrong.*			
	Who are the Indians?	*[most students raise hands to be Indians]*		
	We don't have many Spaniards			
	Indians, you have the floor. Tell how you feel.	*Steven: I would be mad . . .*		
	Spaniard, respond to this.	*Sonja: civilization was not perfect*		
	Divorce yourself from me up here.	*John: Spaniards had no right to take down the gods. You can't see their god . . .*		

Figure 2.5. *Continued*

Insights From the Research

For the reader's convenience, the following citations are organized under similar headings as used in the chapter.

The Preobservation Conference

- Richard Manatt (1988; Manatt, Palmer, & Hidlebaugh, 1976) suggested that before the observation, the teacher and observer identify the nature of the lesson, make objectives explicit, discuss what the teacher will be doing, and predict what the students will be doing. This conversation sets the agenda for the conversation following the lesson as well.

- According to Shirley Stow and Jim Sweeney (1981), the Preobservation Conference should address objectives of the lesson, materials to be taught, teaching procedures, and unusual behaviors to be observed.

- Julian Prince (1983-1984) had referred to the information gleaned by the observer during the preconference as insights into what the teacher is expecting to accomplish.

- Keith Acheson and Meredith Gall (1987, 1999) described this meeting as the planning conference not only for the lesson but also for the entire relationship between the observer and observee. The nature of the lesson is predicted, including what the teacher intends to do and how the students are intended to respond.

- Thomas McGreal (1988) actually correlated the usefulness and reliability of the entire observation with the integrity of the preconference. He insists that the usefulness and reliability of classroom observations are directly related to the amount and type of information that the observer has prior to the observation.

- Andrew Gitlin and Karen Price (1992) saw the preconference as an opportunity to thoughtfully consider with one's partner the appropriateness of teaching decisions to the goals and contexts of instruction. In their judgment, the intentions set forth in the preconference actually became the text for later analysis.

- In the preobservation discussion preferred by Patricia Holland, Renee Clift, and Mary Lou Veal (1992), the teacher tells the observer what information to collect. This frames the lesson in context before it begins and sets the stage for reflection after it occurs. To a large extent, the lesson is a microcosm of the teacher's entire class plan.

- James Nolan, Pam Francis, and Brent Hawkes (1993) described the preconference as a collaborative work session in which teacher and observer determine the intended teacher actions and anticipated student outcomes. Specifically, they should discuss the content to be taught, the compatibility of instructional strategies with content objectives, and which beliefs about the content and the learning process are being conveyed.

- In describing the CADRE program of collaborative peer assistance, Lyndon Searfoss and Billie J. Enz (1996) identified the frequent and substantive dialogue among teachers about instruction as the central mechanism of the system. The more regularly and honestly colleagues share about the teaching-learning process, and the more feedback they seek from each other, the more legitimately they grow as professionals.

- Linda Darling-Hammond (1998) has long advocated teacher learning that supports student learning. She suggests professional discourse among colleagues to describe classroom activities that directly affect student performance. This stimulates more thoughtful planning and may actually prevent many mistakes and failures—a much preferred alternative to fixing the problems after they occur.

Objectives

Congruence Among Objectives, Teaching Strategies, and Testing Techniques

- Ralph Tyler (1950) has generally been considered the originator of the idea of congruence or "triangulation" among objectives, teaching techniques, and assessment strategies. His "Tyler Triangle" has become one of the icons of curriculum studies in most colleges of education. Until his death in the mid 1990s, Dr. Tyler continued to cite research documenting that a lack of fit between any two of the three components diminished learning success, even among the most capable students.

- In the OERI-commissioned review of successful instructional reforms, Ronald Anderson (1995) identified congruence—or "complementarity"—as one of the critical components of successfully improving classroom delivery.

- Mark Baron and Floyd Boschee (1996) described the relationship among the intended outcomes, teaching methods, and assessment strategies as the most crucial determiner of whether and how much the written curricular reform has any actual impact on student outcomes.

- In reporting on school reform in North Carolina, Joseph Peel and C. E. McCary III (1997) detailed the importance of congruence or triangulation among the curricular objectives, teaching methods, and assessment techniques as the crucial link between curriculum and instruction. In their judgment, this relationship clarifies the standards of quality in all student accomplishments.

Selecting or Developing
Unit Objectives

- James Beane (1995) insisted that unit objectives be tied to prior and subsequent learning to achieve a viable segue between the two. This "before-during-after" effect also helps a teacher see how each unit fits into the school year and defines its pertinence to the whole.
- Robert J. Sternberg (1997), learning theorist and IBM professor at Yale, suggested that various levels of mental processing be built right into teaching objectives and require students to use memory, analysis, creativity, and practicality.
- Since 1956, and again in 1971, Benjamin Bloom has urged teachers to include multiple levels of thinking and problem solving in each unit's objectives (Bloom, 1956; Bloom, Hartings, & Madaus, 1971). This is not to suggest that all six levels of Bloom's Taxonomy must be present in every unit, nor that every concept in the unit must progress from Knowledge through Evaluation. The idea is to provide a sampling to give students a wide array of different level activities in alternate contexts.
- Several of the most highly respected educational scholars associated with thinking skills have contributed to the model as well. These include Art Costa's (1985) work in developing minds; Costa's work in cognitive coaching with Robert Garmston; Hilda Taba's (1966) methods for inductive mental processes and using categories; and David Perkins and Gavriel Saloman's (1989) work in using higherorder thinking to merge process with content.
- Lorna Earl and Paul LeMahieu (1997) insisted that all students be able to think critically, solve problems creatively and independently, make informed judgments, and discern the appropriate course of action from ambiguous situations. If this is to occur, such experiences must be guided by teaching-learning objectives that require students to do so; it will not happen by chance, and it will not automatically transfer from lower-level objectives.
- The president of Boston's Institute for Responsive Education, Tony Wagner (1998), noted that the adoption of more rigorous

performance standards was the easy part. Translating them into measurable learning objectives and establishing the game plan for instruction were the truer tests of whether a district could actually accomplish reform.

Motivation

- Constructivists Jacqueline and Martin Brooks (1993) suggested several types of questions—and parallel means for delving—to ask at the outset of a unit to determine students' levels of readiness and to help the teacher with subsequent planning. If students are to construct much of their own learning, the question-answer scaffold will generalize to various learning constructs.

- Joan Palmer (1995) and James Beane (1995) each insisted that motivational activities connect current unit objectives to both the previous and subsequent units to provide students a frame of reference.

- Noted assessment specialist Grant Wiggins (1996) argued that samples of the kind and quality of work required should be provided students at the outset of the unit. His intent is that students are never blindsided by the expectations or evaluation criteria, and this is ensured when they know from the very beginning where they are expected to be by the end.

- The Director of the Center for Policy Analysis at Rutgers, William A. Firestone (1997b), compared American education with that of the United Kingdom and determined that U.S. students have too few opportunities to analyze why things are the way they are. Students need to look for connections among topics, ideas, and principles and to address issues that may be personally meaningful as well as those things for which they will be held accountable. There is a definite need to personalize learning activities.

- Linda Darling-Hammond and Beverly Falk (1997) suggested that students need to feel successful at something they know, followed quickly by success at something new. This cycle generates intrinsic motivation or self-renewal to balance the external motivation exerted by teachers and parents. In a later article, Darling-Hammond (1998) explains that the skillful teacher knows how to make ideas accessible to students; he or she figures out what students know and believe about a topic and how they can best hook into new ideas.

The Delivery of Information

- Lorrie Shepard's (1989, 1995) work has been among the most frequently cited in conjunction with constructivism; she contrasts it with what she calls outmoded learning theory—that children learn by the accretion of little bits of information. Shepard's trademark phrase, "meaning-making," is based on her insistence that learners arrive at understanding when they construct their own knowledge and devise their own cognitive maps of interconnections among the facts and concepts being considered. Another phrase associated with constructivism is Robert Sylwester's (1995) "cognitive scaffolding"—a metaphor for learning aids that brace the learner while he or she internalizes or masters the content, and are then taken away once the learning "cement" has dried and stands alone. Sylwester is convinced that these scaffolds can be applied and then removed much earlier and more rapidly than was once believed. Linda Darling-Hammond (1993) referred to "learning schema," Karen Harris and Michael Pressley (1991) alluded to "cognitive strategies," and Ann Brown and Annemarie Palincsar (1988) suggested that "reciprocal teaching," or the teacher and student working together as co-learners, is the best way to teach children how to use the constructs.
- Since 1992, Linda Darling-Hammond (1992, 1993, 1995) has claimed that teachers not only lack a sense of the deep structure of their content areas but also how to select and deploy delivery strategies appropriate to the content and the developmental needs of their students.
- Gordon Cawelti (1995), longtime ASCD chieftain and now a research associate committed to curricular reform, has not veered from the position that the research does not identify one best method or right way to provide instruction. It does not prove that certain instructional practices should always or never be used. But it *has* illuminated which instructional methods are more and less likely to achieve the desired results for specific kinds of content, types of learner, and under what conditions. Two years earlier, Steve Zemelman, Harvey Daniels, and Art

Hyde (1993) had assembled many of these "more and less likely to succeed" methods into lists of best and worst teaching practices associated with school reform.

- Howard Gardner (1991; Brandt, 1993b) agreed with Paul Pintrich (1993) that inauthentic learning occurred when students attempted to mimic or parrot back to teachers what is in the textbook and/or the teacher's own wording. Constructivists Jacqueline and Martin Brooks (1993) refer to authentic learning as generative, active productions rather than passive reception.

- Linda Darling-Hammond and Beverly Falk (1997) insisted that successful teachers offer challenging, interesting activities that are guided by rigorous standards and high expectations. Among the strategies that accomplish this are demonstration, lecture, individual work, performance assessments, group activities (some collaborative and some cooperative), and peer tutoring.

Assessment

- As a result of their investigation of teaching practices, Richard Stiggins and Nancy Conklin (1992) concluded that better assessments will drive instruction, but only if teachers can (a) distinguish valid from invalid tests—especially among so-called teacherproof published tests—and (b) integrate assessment with instruction rather than wait until the end as if it were separate from the learning process.

- Stanford Professor J. D. Krumboltz and research fellow C. J. Yeh (1996) said that the reformed assessment is diagnostic, helping the student, the parent, *and* the teacher determine what has not yet been mastered and which intervention might be in order. Enlightened teachers realize that failing a large number of students does *not* signify high expectations and rigorous performance standards. Rather, it attests to poor teaching and insensitivity to the learning needs of students. This is not to water down standards. Low-ability students must be challenged to think at higher levels than has been customary, and high-ability students must demonstrate even higher levels of thought—the idea is not *more* work, but work at greater depth.

- Rutgers mathematics and science professor George Pallrand (1996) reminded teachers that students cannot answer questions for which they have not been given the information and the skills to apply it.

- In her book, Charlotte Danielson (1996) suggested that effective teachers continuously provide students with progress reports, including both constructive and affirmative feedback to help them distinguish when they are on the right track from when they are in error.

- In their work with school reform in North Carolina, Joseph Peel and C. E. McCary III (1997) discovered the importance of diagnostic feedback to guide instructional delivery—well before the high-stakes testing. Many years earlier, Madeline Hunter (1984) likened this formative assessment to wet cement, noting how much easier it was to reshape and resmooth before it became permanent.

- Edgar Schuster (1998), Penn State English Professor and member of the Pennsylvania State Writing Advisory Committee, claimed that nothing would better serve educational reform in the United States than for teachers to accept the fact that the results of their tests measure their own performance as well as that of the students. Thoughtful analyses of their own tests would make teachers far more self-conscious of the decisions they make about assessments. Rather than approaching the assessment process with the traditional paper-and-pencil test— what Schuster likens to one arrow in their quivers—teachers should arm themselves with multiple means for assessing student performance. In addition to determining what students still need to know, the conscientious teacher uses test results as a check against his or her own teaching competence.

- Tony Wagner (1998), president of the Institute for Responsive Education in Boston, sees assessment as a major component of school reform. The author of *How Schools Change: Lessons From 3 Communities,* Wagner insists that formative classroom assessments be diagnostic if they are to be really helpful in contributing to meaningful change. James Popham (1998), the one-time guru of behavioral objectives, admits that objectives are useless without valid and diagnostic assessments. If the tests are carefully crafted and are criterion referenced to the learning objectives, they will bring about truly worthwhile improvements in teaching.

Culmination

- Vito Perrone (1994) referred to intellectual engagement—the involvement of students in defining the scope and character of their learning activities and having them suggest alternate forms of expression, take an alternate point of view on an issue, create original documents and exhibits, and become directly involved in a public service or political event.

- The movement to increase authentic or performance assessment received considerable impetus from the National Commission on Testing and Public Policy (1991). In reaction to mounting criticism from the profession and the public alike, the Commission urged school districts to design valid, accurate, and predictive assessments that would ask students to supply answers, perform observable acts, demonstrate skills, create products, and compile portfolios.

- In his book on expanding student assessment, Vito Perrone (1991) suggested that the trend toward authentic assessment actually began with John Dewey's "exhibits of learning" and "experiential, life-based learning" (1933, 1956). Perrone claims that the theoretical base for authenticism was to place the assessment in a naturalistic setting compared with the inferential context of the traditional test.

- Grant Wiggins (1992) suggested criteria for making performance assessments valid: (a) The task must be authentic and meaningful, worth mastering, or what Bill Spady (1994) would call "significant," because nothing is gained by including assessments that are easily accomplished but of little consequence; (b) the tasks should be a valid sample from which generalizations about academic performance can be made; (c) the scoring criteria should correspond to instructional outcomes or objectives, not arbitrary cut scores or provincial norms; (d) the tasks must ask students to locate, analyze, and draw conclusions about information; (e) students should have some degree of choice and responsibility for deciding how to accomplish the task; (f) students must work in teams to accomplish at least part of the task; and (g) the results must be reported to all stakeholders.

- Constructivists Ron Marzano, Deborah Pickering, and Jay McTighe (1993) saw authenticism as a countermeasure against the "minimum competency" or "back-to-basics" movements of the 1970s. The replacement of some traditional testing with real-life, hands-on assessments will have the effect of increasing expectations and producing more divergent learning outcomes than can possibly occur with narrow, prescriptive, low-level skills tests. Authentic assessments result in tangible products or observable performances that verify the mastery of both content and process objectives, supplementing, not supplanting, traditional paper-and-pencil measures.

- Robert Rothman (1996), Senior Associate of the National Alliance for Restructuring Education, described a standards-based instructional materials program that focused on getting students more fully engaged in the learning process. Each unit was accompanied by one or more final products or authentic performances that correspond to those academic standards addressed by the unit. Collectively, the units represented all of the academic standards adopted by the district.

- In describing lessons from the past and prescriptions for the future, Tom Guskey (1996b) reminded teachers to make authentic assessments an integral part of the instructional process rather than an add-on.

- Fred Newmann (1996) warned testing reformers that if performance assessments were not directly connected to the content standards adopted by school districts, and that if these standards were not translated to daily classroom activities, the results would be disappointing. Assessments for the high-stakes outcomes would remain traditional, with students continuing to reproduce learning as expressed by someone else. Meanwhile, the authentic or performance assessments, although inestimably more memorable and representing the production learning, would remain detached from the real business of classroom instruction.

- Rick Gordon (1998), the Director of Education by Design, a critical skills program of best practices relative to instructional reform, promoted what he calls the experiential learning cycle. He acknowledged that real-world problems are messy, uncertain, and complex, and they may involve "nuanced judgment." But he suggests stepping back to move forward. Students need to actively solve the everyday problems of living and earning a living, and not merely work exercises from a textbook. He teases about the "graveyard" model of teaching—everyone in rows and dead" (p. 391). Mr. Gordon suggests using Ernest Boyer's "human commonalities" as the basis for authentic assessments to measure deep-level performance of skills: (a) the human life cycle; (b) command of symbols; (c) understanding the social web; (d) connections among the scientific, technical, and natural world; and (e) interdependence among individuals and the larger community. To verify mastery, students should prepare exhibits or displays and reflect on their learning either verbally or in writing.

- Tony Wagner (1998) suggested that as students move into the 21st century, they must be equipped to construct their own learning from what they discover in authentic performance assessments. If this is to occur, they must have parallel experiences during their school years in a risk-free atmosphere where they learn to approach quandaries, frame insightful questions, and inquire to find the answers. Most important, they must see that teachers not only value such activities but also demonstrate this level of learning themselves.

The In-Class Data Collection Process

- In describing how much detail should be captured during the observation of a lesson, Ronald Lamb and M. Donald Thomas (1981) insisted that the work situation and the interaction with students be included.

- Thomas Good and Jere Brophy (1984) reminded observers that the teacher's behavior or technique cannot really be examined independent of its effect upon students. The data collected must include both teacher behavior and student response, not one or the other alone.

- Daniel Duke and Richard Stiggins (1986) described the goal of the classroom observer as drawing a representative sample of teacher performance from which conclusions can be made about teacher competence. The observer must be proficient with the tools of description to record the chronology or narrative of events as they unfold.

- Madeline Hunter (1988) emphasized the importance of script-taping an episode of teaching and then analyzing that script to identify and label teaching behaviors that have a high probability of increasing or interfering with student learning. Using the script-tape analysis, the evaluator can plan for the Postobservation

Conference. In Ms. Hunter's view, the script is a diagnostic instrument from which professional growth is reinforced or prescribed. Because the script reflects what did occur, not what should have occurred, it accommodates any teaching style or instructional mode.

- Thomas McGreal (1988) insisted that the data collected during a classroom observation be recorded descriptively rather than judgmentally.

- The National Association of Elementary School Principals (NAESP, 1988) advised that during classroom observations, enough information should be captured to reconstruct the major events of the lesson to a third party. The observer should be able to reveal how the teacher functions, not simply give impressions or judgments. This means that what must be recorded are specific teacher behaviors and student responses.

- James Nolan, Pam Francis, and Brent Hawkes (1993) contended that in collaborative appraisal, In-Class Data Collection is transformed from documenting teacher behaviors using a checklist to the simultaneous capture of information about the people or actors in the lesson as well as many contextual details of the room. These data are necessary for the peer partners to make informed decisions about what thinking processes are occurring in the minds of the students.

- In their analysis of the collaborative observation process, Judith March, Karen Peters, and Heidi Adler (1994) noted the popularity of the modified script-tape to capture the events of the lesson observed. Although other formats are preferable for specific targets (e.g., tallies for the number of times something occurs, or sociograms to document interpersonal communications), the script seems especially suited to the wide-angle snapshot required of most collaborative appraisals.

- Linda Darling-Hammond (1998) advocates teacher learning that supports student learning and suggests observing the practices of other teachers as one method of authentic learning for teachers. By studying the strategies and techniques in action in the context of student outcomes, teachers are provided a forum for reflection and analysis. Ms. Darling-Hammond encourages districts to provide structured opportunities for teachers to observe and analyze each other's teaching behaviors as they affect student performance.

Chapter 3

ANALYZING DATA FOR THE POSTOBSERVATION CONFERENCE

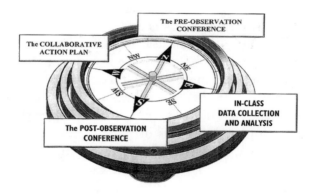

In the COMPASS model, the data collection portion of the collaborative observation process is the all-important first step. Both the Preobservation Conference and In-Class Data Collection are descriptive in form and substance. The Preobservation Conference captures what the teacher intended to occur in the entire unit as well as the actual lesson. As a planning document, the Preobservation Conference form is designed to reflect the best practices that comprise the district's instructional reform initiative. The In-Class Data Collection describes what actually did occur during the lesson and documents the implementation of these reform practices. The next step is for the observer to prepare an analysis of the data collected and to plan for the Postobservation Conference. During this conference, the observer and the teacher will collaboratively reflect on the lesson and devise an Action Plan for growth.

Lesson Analysis

The lesson analysis is recorded directly on the script pages, and each point of analysis is deliberately placed beside the event to which it refers. If there is a definitive pattern in certain behaviors, the teacher can examine the various contexts in which they were repeated. The format for each point of analysis is deliberately structured to avoid subjective judgment. Each analytic point, the positive as well as the questions and concerns, specifies both the teacher behavior and its impact on students. There is a tendency for the beginner to include value or quality words in the analysis statements (e.g., "good rapport," "excellent questions," "poor response to student answer," etc.). Although it may seem more direct, it is evaluative rather than descriptive. It is equally tempting to include prescriptions for areas that are concerns and questions (e.g., "You should have gone to check on the group of students that was off task," "Try to ask higher-level questions," or "It would have been better if you grouped the students in cross-ability groups"). Observers new to the process must be reminded that the prescription comes later and not during this data collection phase. The following excerpt from a script (Figure 3.1) serves to illustrate how the analytic remarks are drawn from the script.

In the analysis statements that follow, the bold type indicates the teacher behavior, and the bold italics refer to the impact on students or the student response.

Two "strengths" might be phrased as the following:

The teacher-developed bulletin board of sculpture examples *provides students with a concrete referent for the criteria of each period (helpful for their projects)*.

Assigning students to create a sculpture as per the characteristics of the period *is an authentic way to assess their understanding of how that one period is distinct from other periods*.

LESSON DESCRIPTION		
Time	Teacher Behavior	Student Response
12:43	bulletin board of sample pictures; passes out study guide while talking Lecture: Types of Sculpture Primitive Sculpture on board behind me; the art was simple, crude, magical beings	students not all in seats when teacher starts; they are talking as the study guide is distributed
12:47	Your project . . . create own sculpture . . . from one of the periods . . . use criteria of that period . . . Egyptian, Greek, Roman "maybe should take a few notes here" Egyptian Sculpture . . . death; Greek/Roman . . . also called Classical Period	a few students chatting; asking each other what teacher said; asked when project due
12:55	[squints to read study guide] asks students if they can read study guide . . . should be clearer That's Baroque (spells for students); I'll explain it later . . . That's Renaissance Impressionistic (spells for students)	students ask questions about what #7 says Student Student asks about #10

Figure 3.1. Excerpt of Script: Grade 9—Art I

A "question" might be written as the following:

> **How did giving directions to take notes after beginning the lecture** *affect students' recording the detail for the earlier periods?*

A "concern" might read:

> **The print of the study guide was broken up and pale,** *the students* *were distracted, and their persistent questioning about how*

The COMPASS Model   *IN-CLASS DATA COLLECTION*

Classroom Drawing						
		Map				
Teacher Desk	*Teacher*				*Table*	
					(books, fliers)	
2 absent						
Linda	*Trevor*	*Susie*	*Beth*	*Troy*		
Peter✓	*Bert*	*Bob*	*Max*	*Steven*✓		
Sonja✓	*Lori*	*Chris(male)*✓✓	*X*	*Heather*		
Bill	*John*✓✓	*Iris*	*Will*	*Sam*		
Jim	*Lucy*		*Melissa*	*Danielle*		
X						

Observer: __*Sample*__

Teacher Observed: __*Dan*__

Materials: __*supplemental texts, notebooks, notecards*__

_____

_____

Date: __*10/17*__   Number of Students: __*23*__

	Lesson Description		Lesson Analysis	
Time	Teacher Behavior	Student Behaviors/Responses	Strengths	Concerns/Questions
8:05	*Aztecs . . . American Indian Race reviewed words from Nahuatl that are still used today*		*relating Aztec vocabulary to modern language provides real-life context for students*	
	City Life			
	City name - Tan . . .	*[students give correct response as a group]*		
	Build on Lake _____			
	How many people did Cortez have? Close. 600	*Chris: 500!*		*levels of question prompted only low-level answers; did not force students to stretch*
	Religion			
	Prisoners			
	Sacrifice			
	Spelled name of god (I could not get it down)			
	volcanic/knife			

Figure 3.2. Completed Script With Analysis   *(continued)*

to spell words coming later on the study guide broke up the flow of the lecture.

There are times when a teacher's behavior or strategy is both a strength and a concern. For example, the study guide in the lesson above was a positive practice, but it was so illegible that it actually distracted students rather than assisted them. We call this a "bow-tie," because it draws from both the strength and the concerns of the analysis. An example of this bow-tie effect is illustrated on the second page of the script for the fifth-grade World Studies lesson in Figure 3.2.

This lesson was a final review of the unit before the assessment and culmination activities, and most of the questions were low-level fact recall. The addition of any questions to make the students stretch or think at a higher level was commendable, but the teacher failed in two

Observer:_____　　　Page:___*2*___

	Lesson Description		Lesson Analysis	
Time	**Teacher Behavior**	**Student Behaviors/Responses**	**Strengths**	**Concerns/Questions**
	What if they sacrificed and they still had eclipse?	*Chris: they didn't sacrifice enough*	*higher-order question prompted students to extend, apply knowledge**	
	plumed serpent . . . *Why did Montezuma fear him?* *What else?*	*Pete: Quetzequala (sp)* *fair skinned*		
	Was he driving a Chevrolet?	*[laugher!!]* *riding a horse (several say)*	*use humor, gets students' attention*	
	Montezuma made big mistake *Cortez figured there was more*	*[students as group] gave him the gold*		
8:13	*[showed article from magazine with Aztecs. Held up pictures for class to see.]*		*including supplemental materials expands textbook-only treatment of subject*	
	Pyramids *What is outstanding about their pyramids?*	*John: they had no machines to move the rocks*	*higher-order question**	*failed to build on higher-order student response; did not elaborate or extend with additional higher-order questions; discourages responses that are not fact-level?* *
	How big? *20 stories*			
	Any questions?			

Figure 3.2. *Continued*　　　　　　　　　　　　　　　　　　*(continued)*

of three instances to elaborate on the student's answer or to draw out other responses that would have taken several students beyond mere recall of the information given. These two opportunities to help students construct a deeper level of understanding were lost.

This sample analysis illustrates the importance of placing each analytic comment directly beside the lesson event to which it refers. It enables the teacher to appreciate the number of times an event or behavior occurred, to understand the various contexts in which it was repeated, and to see what immediately preceded an event. Placed beside the event, the analytic remark also helps reveal patterns in both teacher behavior and impact on students.

The strict adherence to including both the teacher behavior and the impact on students has an important effect on the quality of the analysis. If the observer cannot identify one part or the other, that

Observer:_____   Page:___3___

Lesson Description			Lesson Analysis	
Time	Teacher Behavior	Student Behaviors/Responses	Strengths	Concerns/Questions
	They had schools outstanding students became priests; average students were in houses of youth. Most of us are average, a few would be priests.			*what message may be conveyed to students about what you perceive as their ability?*
8:20	*Now, something interesting. We will find out who is right and who is wrong.*			*setting the tone of "right/wrong" eliminates the possibility that both sides could have a viable position*
	Who are the Indians?	*[most students raise hands to be Indians]*		
	We don't have many Spaniards			
	Indians, you have the floor. Tell how you feel.	*Steven: I would be mad . . .*	*teacher attempted a strategy that would allow students to show their understanding of unit content; your restatement of student comments sparked next comment; you remained neutral to give both sides dignity*	*students' lack of prior experience with/knowledge of debate prevents their knowing how to respond; you kept having to step in*
	Spaniard, respond to this.	*Sonja: civilization was not perfect*		
	Divorce yourself from me up here.	*John: Spaniards had no right to take down the gods. You can't see their god . . .*		

Figure 3.2. *Continued*   *(continued)*

remark cannot be included in the analysis. The most frequent error among beginners is to identify teacher behaviors without connecting them to a positive or negative impact on students. For example, "the level of questions asked by the teacher" does not specify the impact on students. Unless the teacher's actions had an identifiably positive or negative effect, it is usually more a matter of style or personal preference. Conversely, if the observer identifies student responses that *can* be attributed to the teacher's behavior, but the observer does not make the connection, then the analytic remark will be of little value to the teacher. For example, to simply say that "the students were off task during an activity" is not really helpful without the context in which it was happening. This is critical to the teacher who is trying to distinguish those strategies that work from those that do not in terms of their impact on students.

	Lesson Description		Lesson Analysis	
Time	Teacher Behavior	Student Behaviors/Responses	Strengths	Concerns/Questions
8:25	*I think that is terrific, John!! Class, he got deeper . . .* *[elaborated on John's comment] -- focused on feelings, touching, seeing* *[then turned to other supplemental books with information on Aztecs] Read about the women . . .*	*[students browsed through books]*	*reinforced deeper-level thinking; encouraged the student and sent message to other students that they too should try to stretch*	
8:50	*[bell]*			

Observer: _____ Page: __4__

Figure 3.2. *Continued*

The analysis remarks represent the final step in the data collection process. They are now prioritized and transferred to the Postobservation Planning Form.

The Postobservation Conference Preparation

In our experience, planning for the Postobservation Conference is the most consistently neglected aspect of any observation process. Inexperienced observers typically assume that because they have amassed such a convincing array of data, they can hold a postconference without advanced preparation. The COMPASS model actually splits the Postobservation Conference into two parts: planning and delivery. The delivery culminates in the Action Plan and will be treated in Chapter 4. We deliberately include the planning process here in the analysis chapter as a way to synthesize the data collected during the Preobservation Conference, in-class scripting, and lesson analysis.

In the COMPASS model, the Postobservation Conference form is actually a lesson plan for the conference itself (see Figure 3.3). Because the conference is generally limited to 20 or 30 minutes, the observer must prioritize his or her remarks to exchange the most useful information. The initial decision to be made by the observer must be what he or she hopes will be the result of the Postobservation Conference—what the teacher will do differently as a result of having participated in the collaborative observation process. Contrary to many collaborative models, such superficial outcomes as "feel better about herself" or "continue the fine job of . . ." are strictly off limits. Acceptable outcomes specify both a teacher behavior and an impact on students (e.g., "Preassign groups so that students know the arrangement in advance and are able to move without guessing which arrangement is required for a specific activity"). The foundations of the COMPASS model are the best practices of instructional reform and continuous professional development. Therefore, it is not a deficiency model to be used with only struggling teachers. It is during the Postobservation Conference that all teachers—with greater as well as lesser expertise—buy into at least one strategy for growth.

Once the intended result of the conference has been determined, the second decision is what to share during the conference. Unlike traditional evaluation, where the observer uses position power to control the conference and its outcomes, this collaborative process must have a reciprocal dialogue about what occurred during the lesson and a mutual resolution about next steps. As the "other set of eyes," the observer takes the initiative to lead the conference, but both partners must have equal input for the process to be successful.

The Postobservation Conference Plan

Item 1: Positive points to be reinforced. From the analytic remarks recorded as strengths on the script, the observer selects two or three to discuss during the conference. The strengths chosen are determined by the intended outcomes for the conference, are stated in terms of

---

The COMPASS Model

POST-OBSERVATION CONFERENCE

1. Positive points to be reinforced during the conference (focus on teacher behavior/impact on students; documentation is in script).

2. Questions or concerns to be addressed during the conference; (focus on teacher behaviors that did not seem to yield the desired student response, or ask questions to clarify a point of which you are unsure).

3. Areas from the Pre-Conference needing clarification, including feedback on items you were asked to observe.

4. Objectives (when the Post-Observation Conference is completed, what behaviors would you hope the teacher will add or delete.)

5. Alternatives - what other activities, strategies, or techniques might also be effective for teaching a lesson such as this.

Figure 3.3. Blank Postobservation Conference Plan

teacher behaviors and impact on students, and are designed to reflect best practices. When planning the Postobservation Conference, one should begin with the positive points or the strengths. If the observer does not start with something positive in the planning, it is very likely that he or she will focus only on the weak points in the lesson. It is important to note that when starting with the positives, one should focus on points that one feels are truly strengths. Sometimes, observers will identify a strength with tongue in cheek, and this is really not appropriate. The observer should be able to draw from the script a strength such as, "The level of questions prompted students to offer complex responses that required more than rote memory."

Item 2: Questions and/or concerns. Similarly, the observer selects two or three concerns or questions from the script to discuss and phrases these in terms of the teacher behavior and impact on students. Here also, the ones chosen are determined by the intended outcomes of the conference. It is important to select items that represent substantive areas for growth that are reasonable and reflect best practices as set forth in the district's instructional reform. Some concerns are easier to correct and afford an immediate success, whereas others are more deeply ingrained and require a longer time to correct. The strength of the partnership and the level of mutual trust affects which areas are selected. Again, an example might be something like, "The level of questions required students to answer in one word or rote memory responses. They did not have to extend or elaborate on information they had been given previously."

Item 3: Areas from the Preobservation Conference. For this item, the observer refers to what has been recorded on the Preobservation Conference form. In addition to Question 12, where the teacher made a direct request for feedback, the observer should reference other questions or concerns that were not clarified through the classroom observation. An example of what might have surfaced during the Preobservation Conference might be something related to the delivery strategies the teacher plans to use, the verbal directions he or she will give to the students, or a particular student or group of students about whom the teacher would like further information.

Item 4: Objectives for the conference. The observer identifies one or two strategies that he or she would like to see incorporated into the teacher's instructional repertoire. Although these objectives usually relate to the concerns/questions identified above with the lesson observed, they need not be limited to this lesson and may refer to a larger or different context within the district's reform agenda. It is particularly important to note that the objectives do not necessarily refer only to deficiencies or needs. Very often, they relate to expanding an area of strength, learning a new method or strategy, or moving beyond the classroom to influence others. The observer may encourage the teacher to attempt another delivery strategy, such as inquiry—allowing students to construct their own meaning with regard to a concept or discrepant event. The strategy should be something that would expand the teacher's level of performance.

The COMPASS Model

POST-OBSERVATION CONFERENCE

1. <u>Positive points to be reinforced</u> during the conference (focus on teacher behavior/impact on students; documentation is in script).
    *   *relating Aztec vocabulary to our language provides real-life context and connection for students*
    *   *including supplemental materials expands textbook only treatment of the subject*
    *   *attempting debate/role-play allows students to demonstrate an authentic knowledge of unit objectives*

2. <u>Questions or concerns to be addressed during the conference</u>; (focus on teacher behaviors that did not seem to yield the desired student response, or ask questions to clarify a point of which you are unsure).
    *   *students' lack of experience with / knowledge of how to debate prevented their carrying it off; you had to keep stepping in*
    *   *the majority of questions were low-level recall; you gave no response to two of the three students attempting to think at higher levels*

3. Areas from the Pre-Conference needing <u>clarification</u>, including <u>feedback</u> on items you were asked to observe.
    *   *so much use of lecture; how appropriate is this for grade 5? Is this typical of all units?*
    *   *students had no working knowledge of debate format and were unable to carry off two opposing points of view*

4. <u>Objectives</u> (when the Post-Observation Conference is completed, what behaviors would you hope the teacher will <u>add</u> or <u>delete</u>.)
    1. *Use debate in another unit, but show students the "how to" before hand; allow them to prepare in advance to increase the quality of their responses.*
    2. *Elaborate on higher-level thinking in student answers by delving or building on the responses and helping other students see the connections.*

5. <u>Alternatives</u> - what other activities, strategies, or techniques might also be effective for teaching a lesson such as this.
    1. *Replace note cards with an overhead of key review points (perhaps an open outline); this will enable you to move among students to encourage their involvement.*
    2. *Have students work in groups to examine the supplemental materials for information that could be used on both sides of the debate.*
    3. *Students could work in teams to devise review questions for each other; show them how to devise higher-order questions and how to respond to the answers by building further connections among unit concepts.*

Figure 3.4. Sample Postobservation Conference Plan

Item 5: Alternatives. It is important for the observer to have identified one or two methods, activities, or strategies that might be equally successful in teaching this type of lesson. This is not to second-guess the teacher about the lesson in reference but to help the teacher expand his or her options when planning future lessons that are similar. When a lesson has been disappointing to the teacher, it is common for him or her to inquire as to alternative possibilities. Because each partner serves as both teacher and observer, this part of the collaborative observation process provides a bank of best practices to improve instruction. Figure 3.4 is a sample Postobservation Conference form for the fifth-grade World Studies lesson.

Although the Postobservation Conference Planning Form serves as the lesson plan for the conference, the observer does not take the completed form into the conference, nor is it shared with the teacher. This planning document represents the observer's personal synthesis of all data collected. It contains more information than is reasonable to share, and it may include comments that will be inappropriate, depending on the teacher's responses.

Insights From the Research

The Lesson Analysis

- Daniel Duke and Richard Stiggins (1986) identified the most crucial interpersonal link between the teacher and observer as that which occurs when the teacher is given information about his or her performance. The feedback must be carefully planned to describe aspects of the teaching itself and its impact on the students.

- The National Association of Elementary School Principals (NAESP, 1988) emphasized the need for the observer to exchange ideas with teachers about how to refine their teaching skills as they affect students to widen their professional horizons. The observer's analysis should include the following: (a) how the students reacted to the teacher's instruction, (b) recurring patterns in the teacher's style that were noted during the observation, (c) specific indicators of how well the lesson accomplished the intended outcomes, and (d) what areas of the teacher's performance need to be reinforced and refined.

- In their discussions of clinical observation, Thomas Good and Jere Brophy (1986) insisted that teacher behaviors should never be appraised apart from their impact on students.

- F. Michael Connelly and D. Jean Clandinin (1988) suggested that student behavior is the most important factor in the teacher's interactive decision making.

- Madeline Hunter (1988, 1993) consistently claimed that the analysis of the interaction between what the teacher does and how the students react is the essence of teacher professionalism. It is only from this analysis, she insists, that those teaching behaviors likely to increase student learning can be distinguished from those most likely to interfere with it.

- According to Andrew Gitlin and Karen Price (1992), the two-way communication between teacher and students and the interpretation of what occurred drive the analysis of a classroom observation. From this analysis comes the direction on how to make improvements and how to generalize to similar situations.

- In direct reference to instructional reform but having implications for the analysis of classroom instruction, Grant Wiggins (1995a, 1995b) insisted that in planning instruction, far greater emphasis must be placed on what makes sense to the learner than on what makes sense to the teacher. It follows, then, that the analysis of instruction should fall along similar lines.

- Lyndon Searfoss and Billie J. Enz (1996) described the CADRE system of peer assistance as providing a forum for frank and honest reflection about which teaching behaviors were more and less successful. Having witnessed the events of the lesson, the observer is positioned to describe the teacher's strategies and how the students responded.

The Postobservation Conference

- More than two decades ago, Dale Bolton (1973) described the following components as necessary for an effective Postobservation Conference, and they have changed very little over time: (a) Establish the purpose for the conference, (b) provide a description of favorable information that consists of honest encouragement rather than vacuous praise, (c) discuss weak aspects of performance, (d) provide for teacher reactions and discussion, (e) determine what additional information may be needed, and (f) discern the next steps to be taken. It is during the postconference that observers establish credibility with the teacher sufficient for them to offer suggestions for areas needing improvement.

- Gary Dunkleberger (1982) pointed out that the Postobservation Conference is often hurried to save time. However, this defeats the purpose of observation and minimizes the potential of the process to help teachers improve their instructional skills. Mr. Dunkleberger reminds the observer that opening the conference by telling the teacher what was wrong is an approach that usually discourages healthy communication.

- Both James Sweeney (1982) and Gary Dunkleberger (1982) insisted that the importance of the postconference requires thoughtful, written planning and adequate time to complete. Without a prepared sense of direction and a clear-cut set of intended remarks, the observer is not likely to get to the major point of the conference, and it will disintegrate into a conversation about issues other than the lesson. Mr. Sweeney feels strongly that the observer must also be alert to the impact of any special biases or circumstances that the teacher brings to the conference.

- Norman Sadler (1982) identified the postconference as the make-or-break point in any performance appraisal system. He contended that the purpose of the postconference is to motivate the teacher to improve job performance, engage in self-development activities, and create a deeper understanding between the observer and teacher.

- The simultaneous importance and sensitivity of the postconference was well-stated by Daniel Duke and Richard Stiggins (1986), who claimed that the most delicate of all interpersonal encounters between two people is when one is giving the other feedback about the latter's performance.

- The National Association of Elementary School Principals (NAESP, 1988) preferred that the teacher receive feedback within 3 days of the observation and that the observer should (a) summarize the purpose of the conference; (b) prepare, in writing, the messages the teacher is to receive from the conference; (c) develop a rationale for statements to be made and refer to specific actions and techniques that were observed; (d) decide on a way to record the teacher perceptions; and (e) be prepared to discuss how to overcome deficiencies.

- Thomas McGreal (1988) suggested that the observer-teacher relationship is affected by the way the feedback is presented. It should consist of examples, anecdotes, illustrations, or descriptions that include what the teacher did and how the students responded. Value statements or value terms should be carefully avoided. Mr. McGreal insisted that the administrator enter the postconference well prepared for the discussion and not attempt to wing it.

- Madeline Hunter (1988) thought that 50 to 100 clock hours of training are needed to develop skill in script-tape analysis and conferencing. She thought that during the postconference, one should focus on (a) what the teacher did to contribute to learning, (b) what alternatives are available if the teacher has another situation, (c) what went the way the teacher anticipated and what the surprises were, (d) what the teacher thought when certain behaviors occurred, and (e) what the teacher would like to select as the focus for instructional improvement.

- According to Keith Acheson and Meredith Gall (1987, 1997), the ideal culmination of the postconference is that both parties agree on what occurred during the lesson and what the next steps should be. The conversation should spring from a set of common assumptions about not only the lesson events but also the desired outcomes. The observer should present the data from the observation with the objectivity of a snapshot, jointly analyze them with the teacher, and reach collaborative agreement on what should come next.

- Andrew Gitlin and Karen Price (1992) suggested placing the events of one lesson against a backdrop of recurrent themes and patterns that have built up over time. Because the conference is informal and private, the teacher is encouraged to share annoyances, disappointments, and frustrations relative to the instructional process. A peer partner is not an evaluator or censor, so the playing field is level, making it much safer to admit areas of weakness.

- Joanne Herbert and Melody Tankersley (1993) described the postobservation conference as a high-stakes discussion between the teacher and observer to analyze interpretively the teacher behaviors and student responses as they occurred during the lesson.

- In an interview with Ron Brandt (1996), Thomas McGreal was asked how realistic most teachers were about the events of the lesson and how prescriptive the observer must be. Mr. McGreal suggested that with the emergence of collaborative appraisal, the intent is to do less prescribing in the conference and more prompting reflection. The teacher will more readily take ownership for correcting less effective behaviors if he or she determines the need.

- Paul Caccia (1996) discussed the importance of trust and confidence in conducting a successful postconference. If the teacher has confidence that the observer has his or her best professional interests in mind, the suggestions made during the conference will be well received. If the relationship is built on reciprocal trust, the observer will gain as much benefit as the teacher from the exchange of ideas.

- As a major principle of teacher learning that supports student learning, Linda Darling-Hammond (1998) suggested that teachers may need training and practice in the collaborative skills necessary to conduct a follow-up conference. The intent of the conference is to help the teacher reflect on what occurred during the lesson and to ask questions that will lead either to validation of successful practice or to positive change if needed. This is accomplished through the medium of collaborative discourse, a form of communication that appears in best practices research as a constructivist strategy for student learning as well.

Chapter 4

DEVELOPING THE COLLABORATIVE ACTION PLAN

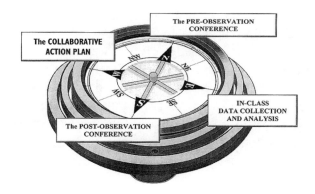

Part 4 of the COMPASS model is the Action Plan, which is jointly developed by the teacher and observer as the culmination of the Postobservation Conference. The Postobservation Conference provides the opportunity for the observer and teacher to reflect collaboratively on the events of the lesson, and the Action Plan is the product of that discussion.

Delivery of the Postobservation Conference

Once the Preobservation Conference and in-class data have been collected, the lesson analyzed, and the plan for the Postobservation

Conference prepared, the observer and teacher hold the Postobservation Conference. Ideally, this should occur within a day or so of the observation. There is not a prescribed format for conducting the Postobservation Conference, but in our experience, the observer generally takes the lead to start the conference and focuses on what the teacher saw as the positive aspects of the lesson.

Strengths

Early in the conference, the teacher is asked which aspects of the lesson went as intended. At the top of the Action Plan Form, space is provided for the observer to record the teacher's response. While doing so, the observer mentally compares what is said with his or her own thoughts about the strengths of the lesson. At appropriate points, the observer interjects his or her perceptions as well. At times, these remarks support what the teacher has said; at other times, they highlight different areas, but the net effect is to validate the teacher for those aspects of the lesson that were successful. The exchange of comments should focus on specific aspects of instruction that reflect best practices and should be described as *teacher behavior* and *impact on students*. An example of a strength that might be reinforced is, "The use of a scoring rubric based on the unit objectives allowed students to see a direct application of the objectives for determining the worth/value of their product."

Questions and Concerns

Similarly, the observer asks the teacher which aspects of the lesson did not go as intended. Again, the observer records the teacher's response and mentally compares what is said with his or her own thoughts. Again, the observer interjects his or her perceptions, tactfully describing what the teacher did that yielded the undesired student response. An example of a question or concern that an observer might raise could be, "How do students determine the value or worth of their product in terms of what was expected of them in the unit?" Notice that the use of a question that yields a *yes* or *no* response is avoided; these questions close the conversation rather than open the discussion. Asking *how* implies that the teacher uses such a practice; but if he or she does not, it opens the door for possible ways to achieve the strategy mentioned. However, there are times when the observer wants to make a more direct, descriptive statement about a teacher behavior that yielded an unwanted student response. Such a concern might be phrased, "Asking Level I questions allowed for students to find the answers in their notes or in the text, but it did not prompt them to think at higher levels, beyond the factual information."

Differences in Perceptions Between the Teacher and the Observer

In our experience, most teachers tend to minimize what they thought went well and magnify what did not. The observer is able to reinforce the teacher with additional points of strength, and is able to allay concerns that not as much went wrong as the teacher might have thought. In the beginning, both the teacher and the observer are naturally wary of what will occur. Over time, and having acted as both the observer and the teacher observed, the partners cultivate a mutual regard for each other's success. These Postobservation Conferences proceed quite cordially, and the discussion leads to additional improvements and enhancements in the classrooms of both partners.

However, there will be occasions when the observer and the teacher do not agree about what aspects of the lesson did or did not go well. In these cases, the conference may become somewhat strained, but with practice and continued development of trust, the outcome can still be productive. When there is a discrepancy between the two perceptions, it is typically that the teacher saw the entire lesson or certain aspects as more successful than did the observer. Although there is no pat dialogue or script for addressing this sensitive problem, the following excerpts from actual Postobservation Conferences may be most helpful.

Scenario #1: Grade 9 Art I lesson on sculpture types (see Chapter 3). The teacher gave a lecture on the periods of sculpture accompanied by a study guide. The guide was pale and illegible, and as a result, students interrupted the flow of the lecture to ask for clarification of terms that were to come later in the lecture. During the Postobservation Conference, the teacher did not see this as problematic but has asked the observer for feedback.

Observer: Actually, the quality of the study guide made your job much harder than it should have been. The students jumped around, asking about the terms and interrupting your lecture. [Note: The observer has phrased the description of what occurred in terms of the teacher behavior and its impact on students, being careful to avoid the use of prescriptive and value words.]

Teacher: Really? I guess I'm just used to it. I've used this for so many years, I guess it's getting worn out. Do you think it's a big deal?

Observer: Yes, I guess I do. Since you didn't get through your lecture, and the students lost their focus, the lesson did not go as well as it could have. [Note: The observer restates the lesson intent and why or how it was aborted.]

Teacher: And so what would you suggest, since I don't have a printer? These kids'll never take notes on their own from a lecture. They can't tell what's important.

Observer: Absolutely. [Note: The observer affirms the teacher's concern.] There are a couple of ideas for how to handle this that we might consider for the Action Plan; these would enable you to convey the information to the students without them getting distracted.

Scenario #2: Grade 6 math lesson on geometric solids. The teacher gave students an explanation about finding the volume of cones and pyramids. He worked several problems on the board and asked for questions. He did not allow adequate time for students to process the information before moving on. Therefore, no students asked questions. During the Postobservation Conference, the teacher did not see this as a problem. In fact, he thought the lesson went quite well because most of the students successfully completed their homework for that lesson.

Observer: Did you have a chance to eyeball the script of the lesson I observed?

Teacher: Yes! Nice job; you really got down everything I said!

Observer: I'm glad you appreciated the detail. Did you notice how many students asked questions or made comments?

Teacher: [looks again at the student response column on the script] Well, let's see . . . well, none. I guess they must have all understood.

Observer: But notice this detail in the student column [points]. When you were working on the board, students were looking at each other's papers, asking questions, whispering, shrugging their shoulders, et cetera. They looked as if they were not getting it. [Note: the description of the teacher behavior and its impact on students.]

Teacher: Gee . . . I didn't realize . . .

Observer: Well, sure. You're working at the board; you don't have eyes in the back of your head. That's one advantage of scripting—I can be another set of eyes. But I know you'd not want the students to leave being unsure of themselves. [Note: again the reference to what the teacher does and how it impacts students.]

Teacher: Oh no! But I can't keep stopping all the time; we've got tons of content to cover . . .

Observer: Exactly! But there are a couple strategies you could use that won't slow you down, but they'll give the students a chance to show you they understand. Plus, the way students copy each other's homework, you'd see who really *does* and doesn't get it before they leave class.

Over the years, we have noticed that in every 10 conferences, the following distribution is fairly typical. In 5 conferences, the perceptions of the teacher and observer are extremely close or even identical. Another 3 are similar to the preceding excerpts; the teacher does not initially recognize a need that the observer has noted. As shown in the excerpts, the observer tactfully draws the teacher's attention to the needs and helps him or her recognize that, if left unaddressed, they could present a major problem. The observer suggests that in the Action Plan, the two of them might structure an alternative strategy or technique—a best practice—to address the need, and they collaborate to make this happen. In the final 2 conferences, the partners begin the collaborative process, but for some reason, one or both shut down as they attempt to work through it. They may feel uncomfortable sharing or simply may not want to invest the time necessary to participate. Some of these people eventually drop out of the process, and we suggest not spending too much time and energy trying to convince them to remain involved. Their reluctance is symptomatic of a deeper concern, and additional pressure either increases their anxiety or further exacerbates their frustration. One teacher was shamed into participating in the process, and when a younger teacher in the department observed him, he deliberately taught a lesson that represented the antithesis of all the school had been working to develop. He would not cooperate in the conferences and refused to take the process seriously. In these cases, we suggest that a district use a more direct approach of corrective supervision through the traditional evaluation process. Everyone humored the uncooperative teacher, but no one wanted to incur his wrath by confronting him directly about his weaknesses.

Development of the Action Plan

At the top of the Action Plan form (Figure 4.1), space was provided for the observer to record the teacher's comments about what went as he or she intended during the lesson and what did not. It is from these comments and the dialogue of the Postobservation Conference that the Action Plan is developed.

Area for Growth

The teacher and observer collaboratively determine an area or two that they feel would be beneficial for the teacher's growth and that reflect best practices as set forth in the district's instructional reform plan. These areas typically represent concerns that resulted from the lesson and/or have surfaced in several lessons, becoming a pattern. The most typical examples that we see include "improving behavior management," "more active involvement by all students," "reducing teacher-centeredness," "increasing the level of questions asked," "providing more constructivist lessons," "increasing the authenticity of assessments," and "providing students an array of choices for completing assignments."

There are times, however, when the teacher prefers to identify an area that is not necessarily a weakness but would be beneficial professionally. It may be a growth goal outside the lesson, such as to prepare instructional materials, develop a training tape, visit other teachers' classrooms, or attempt a new instructional method.

The COMPASS Model

Name:_____   Date:_____   Teacher Observed:_____

Things that went the way the teacher intended; what she/he felt went well and how the students responded	**Things that did not go the way the teacher intended;** what she/he felt did **not** work; and how the students responded

Area for Growth	**Specific Strategies That May Be Tried (begin with a verb . . .)**	**Criteria for Success (so that . . .)**	**Time Frame**	**Role of Support Personnel (if any)**

Figure 4.1. Blank Postobservation Conference Summary and Action Plan

Specific Strategies

In this part of the Action Plan, the partners identify strategies or techniques that the teacher will use to address the areas for growth. We insist on specificity to avoid such vacuous prescriptions as "try authentic assessments" or "improve the amount of student participation" or "raise the level of questioning." Acceptable strategies must directly state *what the teacher will do;* the following examples illustrate this level of specificity:

1. Review samples of authentic assessments [provided by the observer] to identify general criteria; make a list of sample assessments that could be used in this subject.
2. Design assessments that require students to apply unit objectives to solve real-life problems: (a) conduct a survey, assemble the data, and prepare an exhibit that represents an interpreta-

tion of the results; or (b) write a short story that uses the conventions of fiction (dialogue, narration, setting, plot, etc.).

3. Work with students to develop a scoring rubric based on unit objectives to use in evaluating authentic products.

4. Teach students to self-assess their work; assign them to do so on the authentic projects.

5. Replace at least eight whole class activities with group activities: (a) preassign various grouping arrangements (threes, fours, etc.) that students can get into quickly without losing time and that involve them in various combinations; and (b) train students how to work in groups.

6. Assign groups of students to review materials and develop three puzzlements to pose to the rest of the class. Exchange the puzzlements and have groups report on their answers.

7. Ask each student to recap yesterday's lesson by writing a journal entry; have some students read their entries.

8. Classify test and quiz questions as to level of difficulty: Level I: factual recall or memory; Level II: inferential or implied level; Level III: divergent or hypothetical. Ask students to think of higher-order applications or what-ifs.

9. Devise at least five Level II questions and two Level III questions for each class discussion; write them in advance, and begin an entire file to encourage repeated use.

10. Teach students to devise questions at the three levels; use this technique for test review.

Ideally, the Action Plan strategies correspond to the best practices set forth in the district's instructional reform plan. In our experience, districts whose teachers have been involved in instructional reform do not have difficulty in developing the Action Plan and find the strategies helpful in determining what still needs to be refined in their practice.

Criteria for Success

For each strategy or cluster of related strategies, participants must determine how they will know whether a strategy is successful in addressing the area for growth. Beginning each success criterion with "so that . . ." forces participants to connect the teacher's strategies with the proposed impact on students. Frequently, the word after the "so that . . . " is "students," but not always. The sample strategies below are excerpted from the 10 listed previously. These are followed by the criteria for success that should accompany each one.

Strategies:

3. Work with students to develop a scoring rubric based on unit objectives to use in evaluating authentic products.

4. Teach students to self-assess their work; assign them to do so on the authentic projects.

Criteria for Success:
So that students see a direct application of unit objectives as criteria for determining the worth or value of a product; and so that they can compare the quality of their own work to the expectations of the unit objectives.

Strategy:

7. Ask each student to recap yesterday's lesson by writing a journal entry; have some students read their entries; repeat at day's end.

Criteria for Success:
So that the agenda for each day's lesson is important to students; they are compelled to pay greater attention to each day's activity knowing they will be asked to make a journal entry and they may be asked to read their entry; fostering a greater sense of accountability.

Strategy:

9. Devise at least five Level II questions and two Level III questions for each class discussion; write them in advance, and begin an entire file to encourage repeated use.

Criterion for Success:
So that students are prepared to ask and answer questions at various levels of difficulty during class discussions, allowing them to respond at still higher levels on the tests and other assessments.

The COMPASS Model

Name: _Sample_   Date: _10/20_   Teacher Observed: _Dan_

Things that went the way the teacher intended; what she/he felt went well and how the students responded	**Things that did not go the way the teacher intended:** what she/he felt did **not** work; and how the students responded
• students really knew their material • students were excited about the debate; they all wanted to be Indians • students used my materials! . . . they seemed to appreciate the brochures and posters	• not many students raised their hands to answer my higher-level questions • the students just couldn't get into the debate (role-play); only a couple said anything

Area for Growth	Specific Strategies That May Be Tried (begin with a verb . . .)	Criteria for Success (so that . . .)	Time Frame	Role of Support Personnel (if any)
Higher-level questions: • ask more • extend answers	1. Classify test and quiz questions as to level of difficulty (Level 1: factual recall or memory; Level 2: inferential or implied level; Level 3: divergent or hypothetical; ask students to think of higher-order applications; what-ifs). 2. Devise at least five Level 2 questions and two Level 3 questions for each class discussion; write them in advance and begin an entire file to encourage repeated use. 3. Build on student responses by asking another student to expand the response; connect higher-order responses to modern day life.	1. Students value higher-level questions and see a reason to listen to each others' responses 2. Students learn to extend each others' responses and connect them to each other	next unit	Show observer the written questions (samples)
The 'Debate': • actually hold a debate • more students participating	1. Show students how to plan for and conduct a debate (e.g., pro/con; taking a position, rebuttal, etc.). 2. Have students prepare both sides of the debate as if they may present either. 3. Remove yourself from the debate to force students to address each other.	1,2. Students give dignity to both sides of the 'debate' and put themselves in the place of Indians and Spaniards 3. Students can react to each other during the debate and not rely on teacher prompts	next unit	Visit another teacher who uses debates; list strategies used by that teacher to make the debate a success Invite the observer back to watch the next debate

Figure 4.2. Sample Postobservation Conference Summary and Action Plan

Once teachers have incorporated the criteria for success into their Action Plans, they have determined the benchmark for measuring their own success.

Time Frame

We have found that even the most well-structured Action Plan strategies will not materialize unless the plan includes reasonable time frames. More important, the observer or another designated resource person must follow up with the teacher through another observation, the collection of artifacts, feedback on written materials developed, or discussion. The follow-up focuses on the teacher behaviors implemented and their impact on students to determine if additional strategies are needed or whether the teacher should continue to refine the proposed behaviors.

Resource Persons

Many Action Plans cannot be successful without the assistance of at least one other colleague or resource person. Most often, it is a media specialist, department or grade-level chair, the observer, a teacher with particular expertise, or even the principal. In addition to providing specific assistance, such as modeling, reviewing materials developed by the teacher, team teaching, or sharing artifacts, the resource person provides moral support and encouragement. This relationship parallels that of diet partners or exercise pals.

The Postobservation Conference and Action Plan for the Grade 5 World Studies lesson appears in Figure 4.2. Note that the top portion of the form reflects the teacher's perceptions about the lesson.

Insights From the Research

Postobservation Conference

- In describing the NCATE accreditation standards for teacher education—and in conjunction with the National Board of Professional Teaching Standards, Arthur Wise and Jane Liebrand (1996) included the explicit standard that the teachers must be able to explain to each other in a reflective dialogue why they decided to use a certain strategy or practice in a particular way and analyze its impact on the students.
- Pauline Gough (1996), editor of the *Phi Delta Kappan,* wrote that if classroom practice is ever to reflect a reformed view of the learning process, classroom teachers must have the opportunity to observe their colleagues using the reforms, followed by frank discussions about what occurred in the context of a supportive, collegial community.
- Lyndon Searfoss and Billie J. Enz (1996) and Stephanie Pace-Marshall and Connie Hatcher (1996) described collaborative observation as the core component in the CADRE system of

teacher appraisal. CADRE works on three principles: (a) dialogue through which teachers regularly and openly discuss teaching and learning, (b) action research or structured inquiry that follows a written plan and involves teachers questioning themselves and each other about the impact of classroom practices on students, and (c) authentic assessment of practice by colleagues seeking advice and counsel from each other. This counsel applies both to the substantive reinforcement for successful practice and to calling into question performance that is unacceptable. Although not a part of the formal evaluation system, the CADRE instruments are a major vehicle for discussion about successful teaching practice, and the CADRE program has brought holistic instruction back to the center of the evaluation process.

The Action Plan

- Richard Manatt (Manatt, Palmer, & Hidlebaugh, 1976) supported the use of three to six improvement targets at one time as the focus of a teacher's instructional improvement efforts. They proposed the development of improvement targets by (a) using a goal to state what the teacher is to do, (b) setting a time limit in which the teacher can reach the objectives, and (c) deciding criteria for measuring a teacher's success in reaching the target.

- Ronald Lamb and M. Donald Thomas (1981) felt that once weaknesses are identified, observers have a responsibility to help improve performance. Without intervention or assistance, even the most collaborative appraisal is neither helpful nor fair.

- Edward DeRoche (1981) reported that the only way to improve teaching was to change teacher behavior. Using the script analysis, the evaluator and teacher should collaboratively generate a plan for growth during the Postobservation Conference.

- Thomas Good and Jere Brophy (1984) contended that the perfect teacher does not exist; professionals can refine existing skills, discard ineffective ones, and develop new tactics. No one will ever be the perfect teacher, few will even be excellent, but all can become better. The vehicle for becoming better is a professional growth plan.

- Guy Klitgaard (1987) insisted that the observer must be well informed about the research on proven strategies if the suggestions he or she makes are to be taken seriously. [Little more than a decade later, the only thing that has changed in that advice is that "proven strategies" have become "best practices."]

- The successful observer should be able to develop an Action Plan on the spot with modifications based on the teacher's needs and responses (Madeline Hunter, 1988).

- Richard Manatt (1988) described the Action Plan as the most potent phase of the observation process, representing a commitment to do something as a result of the postconference. As a collaboratively developed blueprint through which to make improvements, expand the teaching repertoire, or enlarge the scope of an existing strength, the Action Plan serves a dual purpose. Although it is precipitated from the observation of a particular class, its contents may allude to a pattern from several classes or factors outside the classroom that guide a teacher's professional growth over an extended period of time.

- Andrew Gitlin and Karen Price (1992) alluded to the written strategies as the new set of practices that will later be examined for its impact on student learning. Within the safety of the collaborative spirit, the concerns expressed emanate from both feeling and pedagogical thought and may represent as much an affiliation need as a professional one.

- Peter Grimmett (1996) described the role of the supervisor in assisting teachers with their implementation of reform practices. He summarizes the research completed in British Columbia between 1990 and 1994 involving 25 teacher cohort groups. The most authentic teacher-supervisor relationships were those in which supervisors facilitated classroom-based action research projects with teachers inquiring into their classroom practices. The parallel between best practices in the classroom and in professional development was the definitive catalyst for teacher support.

- In describing what she calls teacher learning that supports student learning, Linda Darling-Hammond (1993) insisted that teachers must be able to use different teaching strategies to accomplish various goals. There are several non-paper-and-pencil methods for evaluating students' knowledge, and teachers must be alert to these as well. Once identified, those teaching and assessment strategies chosen comprise a game plan for the next steps.

> The following references are samples of the research we use in the training program for the COMPASS model. As with all of the references cited in this book, participants translate the points made by the authors into strategy and/or criteria statements to represent best practices in developing the Action Plan. As the culminating activity of the Postobservation Conference, the Collaborative Action Plan truly does become what Richard Manatt (1988) calls the teacher's blueprint for professional growth.

- ASCD's O. L. Davis (1998) expressed concern that although hands-on and minds-on learning is all the rage, in his experience, much of it is little more than arts and crafts. Worse, he contended, many otherwise rich and profitable learning activities, such as witnessing a grand jury indictment or visiting the rainforest, are usually followed up with a mindless exercise like "draw a picture of what you saw." He urges reformers to include reflective, contemplative activities that may not be hands-on per se but are minds-on in that they engage students in a learning process rather than merely expose them to an interesting event.

- In their review of the Effective Schools projects funded by OERI, Patrick Shields and Michael Knapp (1997) noted several characteristics shared by those projects that succeeded in raising levels of student achievement. The instructional activities involve students in higher-order reasoning, critical thinking about familiar notions, and analysis of significant phenomena. Students make extensive comparisons between and among ideas and events, devise their own interpretations, and confront problems with more than one solution. In building connections across subject areas and with real-life situations, students are assigned a wide range of learning tasks.

- According to John Anderson (1997), president of the New American Schools Corporation, one of the school reform lessons learned over the past 5 years is the importance of providing and sustaining professional development. It must equip teachers to deliver instruction that matches the higher performance standards required of the students. Teachers must be held accountable for such higher-level practices as more interactive and less didactic presentations, a greater degree of student choice (but accompanied by accountability for follow-through), collaborative investigations of more open-ended and more realistic problem situations, the effective use of primary source documents, and constructivist rather than reductionist displays of learning.

- Elliott Eisner (1997) reminded school reformers that in framing curricular expectations and improving classroom instruction, alternate forms of representation should not be overlooked. "Cognitive artifacts" such as objets d'art, music, and architecture dramatically expand student understanding of math, the sciences, languages, and history. A teacher's instructional repertoire should include requiring students to recover meaning from and convey meaning through these alternate forms of representation. Richard Snow (1997) agreed with Eisner, suggesting that classroom instruction include all of the symbol systems that students would access throughout their lives, not just the preferred numeric, pictorial, and verbal.

- One of the names most closely associated with authentic or performance assessment, Grant Wiggins (1993), joined James Terwilliger (1997) and Joan Anderson, Lynne Reder, and Herb Simon (1996) in sounding a cautionary note. Enthusiasts must be careful not to overstate results. Not all learning is naturalistic and experiential. Much can be learned from the advice of others as well as from the observation and emulation of experts. Problem-solving scenarios may begin as critical thinking and analysis but soon lapse into memorization of the pattern. Once students get accustomed to headwind/tailwind problems or specific probability quandaries, they may replace one empty algorithm for another. In states where performance assessments have taken on high-stakes proportions, a crisis mentality may develop in much the same way as it has for traditional testing. Teachers may just as easily fall prey to "teaching for the test" and revert to extremely traditional teaching methods like drill and practice, mimicry, and memorization—the worst possible contradiction! Wiggins and Terwilliger join Marzano, Pickering, and McTighe (1993) and Linda Darling-Hammond, Jacqueline Ancess, and Beverly Falk (1995) in suggesting that the performance or authentic assessment be one of many factors in determining student mastery.

Chapter 5

Clearing the Hurdles:
Logistics and Challenges

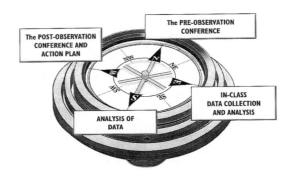

In the field of collaborative observation, there is no shortage of models. Advertised as ready-to-use, with very little training necessary, many models come with their own set of prescribed teacher behaviors or inventories of techniques. Over the years, we have attempted to become knowledgeable about as many of the models as possible. Although we respect and admire some of the well-known collaborative observation systems, we feel that the COMPASS model incorporates the best of several existing programs to monitor a district's instructional reform. Moreover, we had not found a program that used the analysis framework of the teacher's behaviors and their impact on students.

The COMPASS model is designed to be used as a companion to the district's instructional reform program. Ideally, the district has adopted a series of reforms that reflects best practices as documented in the research. Their staff has received professional development in the best practices, and there is an expectation that teachers will use these practices in the planning, delivery, and assessment of instruction. The role of the COMPASS model is to provide the district with a process to monitor these reforms. Teachers are trained as collaborative partners to conduct classroom observations and exchange reflective dialogue about what occurred. The primary unit of analysis in the four-part COMPASS model is the direct relationship between a teacher's behavior and its impact on students.

Training

The logistics for training teachers to participate in the COMPASS model should be collaboratively developed by the trainers and those receiving the training. It is a program where the trainers must have a consistent group of people in attendance for each session. Participants are expected to implement what they have learned between the sessions and prepare write-ups of the work for submission to the trainers.

The training program for the COMPASS model involves a minimum of 24 clock hours of direct instruction typically scheduled across a school year in eight 3-hour sessions. These time frames may vary depending on the group's level of experience. This much time is needed because most participants are not accustomed to observing and analyzing another teacher's instruction. Time must be devoted to conferencing and discussing effective instruction. Over the years, we have determined that someone must conduct *at least* five observations to understand the process and have the necessary level of proficiency with conducting the conferences, analyzing the instruction, and working collaboratively to develop the Action Plan. Although each process can be described simplistically, each requires several hours of practice to fully develop.

The format of the training includes a discussion of the COMPASS model and the research on which it is based, demonstrations of each of the four parts, participant role-plays or simulations of each part during the training, and implementation of each part in the participants' own

COMPASS TRAINING SCHEDULE

Session	Month	Activity	Assignment
1 (3 hrs.)	August	Review of all four parts of the COMPASS model	Select partner for practice observation
2 (3 hrs.)	September	Pre-Observation Conference	Conduct Practice Observation: Pre-Observation Conference and Script of a Lesson
3 (3 hrs.)	September	Scripting and Analysis	
4 (3 hrs.)	October	Post-Observation Conference	Conduct Practice Observation: Post-Conference and Action Plan
5 (3 hrs.)	October	Action Plan	
6 (2 hrs.)	November	Refinement Session: Pre-Observation Conference	Conduct Observation #2 with all four parts
7 (2 hrs.)	January	Refinement Session: Analysis	Conduct Observation #3 with all four parts
8 (2 hrs.)	February	Refinement Session: Action Plan	Conduct Observation #4
9 (3 hrs.)	March	Refinement Session: Action Plan	

Figure 5.1. COMPASS Training Schedule

setting. Consistent with adult learning theory, the eight training sessions are scheduled with 2 to 3 weeks between them to allow adequate time for practice and for reflection and feedback. During the training, participants use teaching lessons on videotape as the basis for their analysis. This allows the consultants to observe the participants as they work through each of the four parts. Because the analysis of the lesson is so important in this process, and teachers have had so little experience doing it, the use of videotaped lessons in the training provides a common reference for practicing data collection and the lesson analysis.

A sample training schedule appears in Figure 5.1.

Planning Details

Flexible schedule. This training schedule reflects 24 clock hours as a minimum, but districts may add hours or sessions as needed. We find that most districts like to offer graduate credit as an incentive, and most universities require 15 clock hours for each graduate credit hour. Extending the schedule to 30 hours would yield 2 graduate hours.

Location.   The physical setting for the training can mean the difference between success and failure. For a number of reasons, the sessions are not taken seriously enough by administrators or staff when they are held at the school building. Staff members tend to take phone calls, to go back to their classrooms, to bring other work to the session, and to not be punctual. The too-familiar surroundings create the impression that what is going on is unimportant. It is far more preferable to hold the sessions off-site in a room with professional conference tables and chairs, audiovisual equipment that works, and refreshments that are attractively presented by someone else.

External and internal facilitation.   It is suggested that district representatives meet with the external consultants to carefully plan the training. Included in their meetings should be representatives of the teachers' union and those people responsible for professional development. The most successful projects, in our experience, have been those where advance planning occurred with all stakeholders present. The union's support is especially critical because any monitoring of classroom instruction may have an impact on teacher evaluation. A discussion of this relationship appears later in the section titled "Challenges."

The role of the *external* consultants is to help the district learn to use the COMPASS model but, more important, to adapt it to local circumstances. The consultants help maintain the big-picture perspective while assisting with the process of working collaborative observation into the district infrastructure as the means to monitor reform results. Even after they complete the training and leave the district, the consultants should maintain contact, perhaps returning once or twice each year to provide reinforcement and encouragement.

The role of the *internal* facilitators is to attend all of the training sessions and fully participate in the classroom observations. Nothing will weaken the program more quickly than if teachers perceive that facilitators are not involved in the process. The people selected as the internal facilitators must be knowledgeable about the instructional reform initiative as well as other professional development programs occurring simultaneously in the district. In addition to the internal facilitators, it is important that at least some of the building principals be involved in the training. Otherwise, they will remain disconnected, and there will never be a cordial or reciprocal relationship between the collaborative observation process and teacher evaluation. After the initial training has been completed, the internal facilitators assume the responsibility for the process. The internal facilitators:

1. Serve as liaisons between the cohort doing the collaborative observation and central office and building-level administrators
2. Arrange for the observations to occur, including the schedule of substitutes, and release time
3. Oversee the collaborative observation process to monitor progress, assess results, and determine the need for adjustments
4. Maintain contact with external consultants when questions arise
5. Recruit additional staff to participate in the collaborative observation process and provide additional training to staff in the COMPASS model

Staff Incentives

Several incentives to encourage staff participation have been used with varying success. These include stipends for time spent beyond the normal school day; graduate credit; release time to participate in training throughout the school day; release from other duties, such as committee assignments; professional development credit toward contractual obligations; and substitutes to cover classes for conferences and observations. Each district must consider its available resources, negotiated agreements, and other staff development priorities. Our experience has been that districts use two or more of the options outlined below in various combinations. It is imperative that the district think of not only the initial training but also long-term implementation in making these decisions.

Stipends

Stipends are one of the most popular incentives, but they are also the most expensive, as the hourly rate for this work is mandated by the contract. The negotiated agreement may also prescribe which teachers must be involved, and these may not be the best candidates for the program. Another risk is that teachers sign up so that they can earn a few extra dollars without really intending to examine their instructional practice. Districts are advised to use a posting process to outline very specific performance outcomes for those who participate. In addition, we suggest that the stipend be a performance contract, specifying that if the teacher fails to follow through with the collaborative observation process, he or she forfeits the stipend dollars.

Graduate Credit

This is also one of the most popular options, especially among less experienced teachers, but veteran teachers are often the most desired participants, and they may not find credit to be an incentive. The key here is that work done on school time may not count toward credit; this is considered double dipping because the teacher is already earning a salary for the teaching day.

Release Time to Participate
Through the School Day

This option is bittersweet; although it eliminates the inconvenience of after school or weekends, teachers often find it too disruptive for their students. Philosophically, many districts resist interfering with instruction, and politically, some communities resent the planned use of substitutes. On the plus side, the cost of subs is usually less than stipends, and because the duty is performed through the school day as part of a teacher's contractual obligation, the district can select its critical mass.

Release From Other Duties

Another popular option among independent schools is to release participants from other duties such as mentoring, coaching, home visits, or committee obligations. In public schools, this may be release from bus duty, study hall, or other nonteaching responsibilities.

Professional Development Credits
Toward Contractual Obligations

Many districts require staff to participate in a set number of professional development hours each year. These hours or days could be used in training for the collaborative observation process.

Substitutes to Cover Classes
for Conferences and Observations

Not actually an option for getting people to be involved in the training, this incentive is a strategy for providing time for teachers to complete the four parts of the collaborative observation process. One strategy is to "timecard" other teachers to cover classes. Another is to hire substitutes who "float" during several key days to release people as needed.

Challenges

As developers and trainers of the COMPASS model, we have encountered various challenges in districts when we meet groups for the first time. Although the process has been presented in a very 'can-do' fashion in the preceding chapters, we would be less than honest if we did not acknowledge some of the issues with which we have had to contend in our work with various districts.

Union Resistance

It would be extremely naive to ignore the teacher association perspective on the collaborative observation process. Until the leadership is assured that the COMPASS model will violate neither their negotiated agreement nor their professional autonomy, there is no point in proceeding. This concern is reasonable in light of past abuses with other reform and professional development initiatives. The ideal way to enlist the cooperation of the union leadership is to involve them from the very beginning in the planning stages and invite them to training sessions. The best way to illustrate this strategy is with two anecdotes.

Anecdote #1. In a large urban district, we had just begun the first training session when one of the participants addressed the entire group. He identified himself as a member of the Executive Board of the teachers' union and made the following statements. Paraphrased, he asked the group members how they became involved in the project and who told them that they had to participate. He sternly reminded them that the collaborative observation process was clearly beyond the expectations of the contract and definitely *not* something they should feel compelled to do. He went on to worry them about abuse and betrayal and reminded them that evaluation was the job of the building principal. Needless to say, we were unsure how to respond, but we allowed him to finish and asked that he reserve judgment until it became clear what was involved in the collaborative observation process. By the end of the training, he was not only an excellent collaborative observer, but he also became one of several teacher trainers who assisted in preparing other teachers in the process. The next year, he was influential in convincing the union's executive board to use the collaborative observation process as the training model for the district's new Peer Review program. Within 2 years, he became a spokesman for the program and visited the teachers' associations in districts that were considering using the collaborative observation process.

Anecdote #2. The Director General of a school board near Montreal, Quebec decided to bring collaborative observation to his district. The first year of his 5-year plan to involve the entire staff was devoted to training his administrative and supervisory team. He also included the leadership of the teachers' union—one from the local chapter and the other from the Province. These two individuals participated in the training with the administrators, completing the observations in district classrooms. Although positive about the process, they wanted to hear about it from a teacher leader's perspective. They contacted one of the union leaders from a district in which we were working and then paid his expenses to visit the district and meet with the teachers to discuss the collaborative observation process.

As conveyed in these anecdotes, the involvement of the union leadership from the beginning is essential if the process is to succeed. This is especially true in situations involving instructional reform, where teachers are expected to use best practices to improve student performance. Once a critical mass of teachers is involved in the process and realizes the mutual benefits of working with peers for professional growth, the program sells itself. We should probably knock on wood at this point, but we have always found this to be the case.

Building Principal Concerns

Another group with a stake in the collaborative observation process is the building principals. Technically, they are to be the instructional leaders of their buildings, and in most districts, they are responsible for teacher evaluation. When we asked prospective principals why they thought reform efforts do not get off the ground, they reported that teachers receive training and are expected to implement the reform irrespective of the building administrator. Without knowing the focus of the reform and the expectations, principals feel disconnected from the reform and, as such, let it go by the wayside.

An understandable concern among principals is that collaborative observation may undermine their authority with the teachers they supervise. This can be avoided if they participate in the training and actually complete the observations as peers rather than as principals. By demonstrating that they can relate to teachers as equals and can give viable, constructive feedback about the teaching-learning process, principals will soon see their authority actually enhanced.

Many districts continue to refer to their principals as the Instructional Leaders of the buildings, but a more enlightened perception is that principals are actually leaders of instructional leaders. This is especially true in districts with instructional reform plans that hold teachers accountable for implementing various best practices. As the leader-of-leaders, each building principal has a strategic role in the instructional reform process and takes it seriously. For example, instruction is the emphasis of faculty meetings, teachers are regularly asked to share their implementation of the reform strategies and how students are being affected, the principal talks to individual teachers about best practices, and he or she includes the collaborative observation behaviors when conducting conferences and classroom observations.

Relationship to Evaluation

In every district where we have worked with the collaborative observation process, one of the initial questions is how it will relate to the present system of faculty evaluation. The COMPASS model is designed to interface with the district evaluation in any one or a combination of the following:

The current evaluation system with the COMPASS enhancement. The current system for evaluation remains as is, and observations completed using the COMPASS model are voluntary enhancements to professional growth. A necessary condition of this level is that the COMPASS results—be they positive or negative—do *not* impact the teacher's official evaluation in any way.

A blend of the current evaluation system with the COMPASS model. One level above keeping the two systems totally separate is the possibility of blending them on one of two levels. The first level represents a blend at the point of offering prescriptions for improvement; the second level incorporates a blend of various aspects of the COMPASS model throughout the evaluation process.

1. The evaluation is conducted using the current system until the conclusion of the Postobservation Conference. At this point, the observer and teacher use the Action Plan from the COMPASS model and collaboratively develop a plan for growth. As per the COMPASS Action Plan format, they identify areas for growth, specific strategies the teacher will use, criteria for success that involve an impact on students, a time frame, and resource people to be of assistance.
2. The evaluation is conducted using the current system, but the evaluator uses some or all of the COMPASS forms to complete each process: the Preobservation Conference, the In-Class Data Collection form, and the Postobservation Conference and Action Plan. The evaluator may still complete the forms required by the official evaluation system—checklists, narratives, and so on.

Replacement of the current evaluation system with the COMPASS model. A third possibility is for an individual teacher to choose the COMPASS model as the means for his or her evaluation. With this option, several observations are completed during the year by the principal and peer partners using the COMPASS model. At the end of the year, the principal, the peer partners, and the teacher prepare a composite evaluation report. It should be noted that because the COMPASS model is not designed to provide summative evaluation data, there is no form for this composite. Some of the districts with whom we have worked added forms or adapted their current evaluation forms to accommodate this option.

Multifactored evaluation system. A fourth option is to use the COMPASS model of collaborative observation as one element in a multifactored evaluation system. This is a popular option in independent schools where we have worked, although it is not considered viable in public schools as yet. In addition to the quality of classroom instruction, independent schools include several correlate areas in their composite performance evaluation of faculty. These include parent and pupil perceptions, professional growth activities, self-assessment, and student achievement. In effect, the culture of the independent school is such that these correlate areas actually enhance the teacher's effectiveness in the classroom. Headmasters and directors of many independent schools encourage faculty to use collaborative observation as the means to establish professional growth targets and as a method of self-assessment.

Regardless of how a district uses the COMPASS model in conjunction with its evaluation, our intent in designing it was to provide a mechanism for districts to sustain their instructional reform initiatives through classroom observation of the teaching-learning process. If districts choose not to use collaborative observation to monitor their reform initiatives, they will miss the opportunity to raise the level of classroom effectiveness and sustain their reform efforts. The formal evaluation system alone cannot provide this type of diagnostic analysis and reflective discussion about instruction.

Summary

Although there are challenges to be faced in the implementation of the COMPASS model, none is insurmountable. The key is careful planning in the beginning. We have found that with the appropriate groundwork, teachers and administrators see this process as one of the most beneficial initiatives they have done for themselves and their students. Otherwise, there simply are not enough hours in the school day for faculty to have professional dialogues about teaching and learning. These opportunities must be structured in order to guarantee that they occur. It is through these reflective discussions that teachers learn from one another and are reinforced for what works with students. The process opens classroom doors that were previously closed.

CONCLUSION

When authors reach the end of a manuscript, they are expected to write a conclusion. But in this case, we really feel that the Collaborative Observation Process to monitor school reform has barely begun. As school districts approach the 21st century, it will not be with instructional programs that were designed for the 1950s or even the 1980s. We know what constitutes best practice and what teachers need to do differently to increase student achievement. We have three decades of research to support the effectiveness of "collaborative appraisal" as the method of choice for sustained professional growth among teachers. The job of putting together the two most powerful ideas in education from the 20th century to carry us into the 21st century just had to be done!

BIBLIOGRAPHY

Acheson, K., & Gall, M. (1987). *Techniques in the clinical supervision of teachers.* New York: Longman.

Acheson, K. A., & Gall, M. D. (1997). *Techniques in the clinical supervision of teachers: Inservice applications* (4th ed.). New York: Longman.

Airasian, P., & Walsh, M. (1997). Cautions for classroom constructivists. *Education Digest, 62,* 62-68.

Alper, L., Fendel, D., & Fraser, S. (1996). Problem-based mathematics—not just for the college-bound: Interactive mathematics program. *Educational Leadership, 53,* 18-21.

Ambach, G. (1996). Standards for teachers: Potential for improving practice. *Phi Delta Kappan, 78,* 207-210.

Anderson, J. (1997, June 18). Getting better by design. *Education Week, 16,* 48.

Anderson, J., Reder, L., & Simon, H. (1996). Situated learning and education. *Educational Research, 25*(4), 5-11.

Anderson, R. (1995). Curriculum reform: Dilemmas and promise. *Phi Delta Kappan, 71,* 33-36.

Anderson, R. (1996). *Study of curriculum reform.* Washington, DC: U.S. Department of Education, Office of Educational Research and Improvement.

Anderman, E. M., & Maehr, M. L. (1994). Motivation and schooling in the middle grades. *Review of Educational Research, 64,* 287-309.

Ausubel, D. P. (1968). *Educational psychology: A cognitive view.* New York: Holt, Rinehart & Winston.

Baker, E. (1993). Questioning the technical quality of performance assessment. *School Administrator, 50,* 12-16.

Ball, G. C., & Goldman, S. (1997). Improving education's productivity: Re-examining the system to get the schools we need. *Phi Delta Kappan, 79,* 228-232.

Bandura, A. (1977). *Social learning theory.* Englewood Cliffs, NJ: Prentice Hall.

Baron, M., & Boschee, F. (1996). Dispelling the myths surrounding OBE. *Phi Delta Kappan, 77,* 574-576.

Barth, R. (1990). *Improving schools from within: Teachers, parents, and principals can make the difference.* San Francisco: Jossey-Bass.

Beane, J. A. (1995). Conclusion: Toward a coherent curriculum. In J. A. Beane (Ed.), *Toward a coherent curriculum: 1995 ASCD Yearbook* (pp. 170-176). Alexandria, VA: ASCD.

Berkson, W. (1997). Place to stand: Breaking the impasse over standards. *Phi Delta Kappan, 79,* 207-211.

Berliner, D. C. (1988, April). *Memory for teaching events as a function of expertise.* Paper presented at the annual meeting of the American Educational Research Association, New Orleans, LA.

Bernauer, J., & Cress, K. (1997). How school communities can help redefine accountability assessment. *Phi Delta Kappan, 79,* 71-75.

Blake, R., & Mouton, J. (1985). *The managerial grid III: The key to leadership excellence.* Houston, TX: Gulf.

Bloom, B. (1956). *Taxonomy of educational objectives: The classifications of educational goals: Handbook 1: Cognitive domain.* New York: David McKay.

Bloom, B. S., Hartings, J. T., & Madaus, G. F. (1971). *Handbook on formative and summative evaluation of student learning.* New York: McGraw-Hill.

Bolton, D. (1973). *Selection and evaluation of teachers.* Berkeley, CA: McCutchan.

Bostingl, J. (1992). *Schools of quality.* Alexandria, VA: ASCD.

Bracey, G. W. (1993). Filet of school reform, sauce diablo. *Education Week, 12*(38), 28.

Bracey, G. W. (1996). Research: What's in it for my kid? *Phi Delta Kappan, 78,* 331.

Bradley, A. (1996). Divided we stand: What has come between the public and its schools? *Education Week, 16*(10), 31-34.

Bradley, A. (1997a). Accreditors shift toward performance. *Education Week, 17*(9), 1, 10.

Bradley, A. (1997b). Fate of peer review rests with NEA locals. *Education Week, 16*(46), 14.

Bradley, A. (1997c). Licensure pact pays dividends for teaching. *Education Week, 16*(34), 1, 28.

Bradley, A. (1998). Unions agree on blueprint for merging. *Education Week, 17,* 1.

Brandt, R. (1993a). On restructuring roles and relationships: A conversation with Phil Schlechty. *Educational Leadership, 51*(2), 8-11.

Brandt, R. (1993b). On teaching for understanding: A conversation with Howard Gardner. *Educational Leadership, 50*(7), 4-7.

Brandt, R. (1996). On a new direction for teacher evaluation: A conversation with Tom McGreal. *Educational Leadership, 53*(6), 30-33.

Bridges, E., & Hallinger, P. (1992). *Problem based learning for administrators.* Eugene, OR: ERIC Clearinghouse on Educational Management.

Brooks, J. G., & Brooks, M. G. (1993). *In search of understanding: The case for constructivist classrooms.* Alexandria, VA: ASCD.

Brophy, J. (1990). Teaching social studies for understanding and higher-order applications. *Elementary School Journal, 90,* 351-417.

Brophy, J., & Good, T. (1986). Teacher behavior and student achievement. In M. Wittrock (Ed.), *Handbook of research on teaching* (3rd ed., pp. 328-375). New York: Macmillan.

Brown, A. L., & Palincsar, A. S. (1988). Teaching and practicing thinking skills to promote comprehension in the context of group problem solving. *Remedial & Special Education, 9*(1), 53-59.

Bruer, J. (1997). Education and the brain: A bridge too far. *Educational Researcher, 26*(8), 4-14.

Bruner, J. (1961). *The process of education.* Cambridge, MA: Harvard University Press.

Bruner, J. (1966). *Toward a theory of instruction.* Cambridge, MA: Harvard University Press.

Bruner, J. (1995). *Man: A course of study.* Cambridge, MA: Educational Services.

Bruner, J., Goodnow, J. J., & Austin, G. A. (1967). *A study of thinking.* New York: Science Editions.

Buday, M., & Kelly, J. (1996). National board certification and the teaching profession's commitment to quality assurance. *Phi Delta Kappan, 78,* 215-219.

Caccia, P. (1996). Linguistic coaching: Helping beginning teachers defeat discouragement. *Educational Leadership, 53*(6), 17-20.

Caine, R., & Caine, G. (1991). *Making connections: Teaching and the human brain.* Alexandria, VA: ASCD.

Caine, R., & Caine, G. (1997). *Unleashing the power of perceptual change: The potential of brain-based teaching.* Alexandria, VA: ASCD.

Cawelti, G. (1995). *Handbook of research on improving school architecture.* Arlington, VA: Educational Research.

Cawelti, G. (1996). A model for high school restructuring. *Educational Forum, 60,* 244-248.

Chase, B. (1998a). NEA's role: Cultivating teacher professionalism. *Educational Leadership, 55(5),* 18.

Chase, B. (1998b, January 21). Still a nation at risk: 15 years later, we're also a nation in denial. *Education Week, 17*(31), 36.

Clinchy, E. (1998, February 4). "Different drummers" and teacher training: Who is out of step with whom? *Education Week, 17,* 72.

Cohen, F., & Seaman, L. (1997). Research versus "real-search": A candid look at restructuring and an alternative path to excellence. *Phi Delta Kappan, 78,* 564-567.

Connelly, F. M., & Clandinin, D. J. (1988). Studying teachers' knowledge of classrooms: Collaborative research, ethics, and the negotiation of narrative. *Journal of Educational Thought, 22,* 269-282.

Costa, A. (1985). *Developing minds: A resource book for teaching thinking.* Alexandria, VA: ASCD.

Costa, A., & Kallick, B. (1993). Through the lens of a critical friend. *Educational Leadership, 51*(2), 49-51.

Coxford, A., & Hirsch, C. (1996). A common core of math for all: Core-plus mathematics project. *Educational Leadership, 53*(8), 22-25.

Danielson, C. (1996). *Enhancing professional practice: A framework for teaching.* Alexandria, VA: ASCD.

Darling-Hammond, L. (1991). The implications of testing policy for quality and equality. *Phi Delta Kappan, 73,* 220-225.

Darling-Hammond, L. (1992). Reframing the school reform agenda: New paradigms must restore discourse with local educators. *School Administrator, 49*(10), 22-27.

Darling-Hammond, L. (1993). Reforming the school reform agenda: Developing capacity for school transformation. *Phi Delta Kappan, 74,* 753-761.

Darling-Hammond, L. (1995). Changing conceptions of teaching and teaching development. *Teacher Education Quarterly, 22*(4), 9-26.

Darling-Hammond, L. (1996). What matters most: A competent teacher for every child. *Phi Delta Kappan, 78,* 193-200.

Darling-Hammond, L. (1998). Teacher learning that supports student learning. *Educational Leadership, 55*(5), 6-11.

Darling-Hammond, L., Ancess, J., & Falk, B. (1995). *Authentic assessment in action: Studies of schools and students at work.* New York: Teachers College Press.

Darling-Hammond, L., & Falk, B. (1997). Using standards and assessments to support student learning. *Phi Delta Kappan, 79,* 190-199.

Darling-Hammond, L., & Sclan, E. (1992). Policy and supervision. In C. Glickman (Ed.), *Supervision in transition: 1992 ASCD Yearbook* (pp. 7-29). Alexandria, VA: ASCD.

Davies, A., & Williams, P. (1997). Accountability: Issues, possibilities, and guiding questions for district-wide assessment of student learning. *Phi Delta Kappan, 79,* 76-79.

Davis, O. L. (1998). Beyond beginnings: From hands-on to minds-on. *Journal of Curriculum and Supervision, 13*(2), 119-122.

Delisle, R. (1997). *How to use problem-based learning in the classroom.* Alexandria, VA: ASCD.

DeRoche, E. (1981). *An administrator's guide for evaluating programs and personnel.* Boston: Allyn & Bacon.

Dewey, J. (1910). *How we think.* Boston: D. C. Heath.

Dewey, J. (1933). *How we think* (Rev. ed.). New York: D. C. Heath.

Dewey, J. (1956). *The school and society.* Chicago: University of Chicago Press.

Dewey, J. (1963). *Philosophy, psychology, and social practice.* New York: Putnam.

Dewey, J. (1995). Science as subject-matter and as method. *Science Education, 4,* 391-398.

di Wijk, S. (1996). Career and technology studies: Crossing the curriculum. *Educational Leadership, 53*(8), 50-53.

Doyle, D. (1997). Education and character: A conservative view. *Phi Delta Kappan, 78,* 440-443.

Duke, D., & Stiggins, R. (1986). *Five keys to growth through teacher evaluation.* Portland, OR: Northwest Regional Laboratory.

Dunkleberger, G. (1982). Classroom observation—what should principals look for? *National Association of Secondary School Principals Bulletin, 66*(458), 9-15.

Dunn, R., & Griggs, S. (1988). *Learning styles: Quiet revolution in American secondary schools.* Reston, VA: NASSP.

Earl, L. M., & LeMahieu, P. G. (1997). Rethinking assessment and accountability. In A. Hargreaves (Ed.), *Rethinking educational change with heart and mind: 1997 ASCD Yearbook* (pp. 149-168). Alexandria, VA: ASCD.

Eggebrecht, J. (1996). Reconnecting the sciences: Integrated science program at Illinois Mathematics and Science Academy. *Educational Leadership, 53*(8), 4-8.

Eisner, E. (1997). Cognition and representation: A way to pursue the American dream. *Phi Delta Kappan, 78,* 348-353.

English, F. (1992). *Deciding what to teach and test: Developing, aligning, and auditing the curriculum.* Newbury Park, CA: Corwin.

English, F., & Steffy, B. (1997). Toward balanced assessment. In *Curriculum and assessment for world class schools* (pp. 67-76). Lancaster, PA: Technomics.

Feldman, S. (1997). When schools fail. *American Teacher, 82,* 5.

Fendel, D., Fraser, S., & Resek, D. (1997). What is the place of algebra in the K-12 mathematics program? *NASSP Bulletin, 81,* 60-63.

Feuerstein, R., & Feuerstein, R. (1991). Mediated learning experience: A theorical review. In R. Feuerstein, P. Klein, & A. Tannenbaum (Eds.), *Mediated learning experiences: Theoretical, psychological, and learning implications.* London: Freund.

Fiedler, F., & Chemers, M. (1984). *Improving leadership effectiveness: The leader match concept* (2nd ed.). New York: John Wiley.

Firestone, W. A. (1997a). Designing state-sponsored teacher networks: A comparison of two cases. *American Educational Research Journal, 34,* 237-266.

Firestone, W. A. (1997b, October 8). Standards reform run amok: What the British experience can teach us. *Education Week, 17*(6), 30, 37.

Fogarty, R. (1998). The intelligence-friendly classroom: It just makes sense. *Phi Delta Kappan, 79,* 655-657.

Fullan, M. (1992). School snapshot: Focus on collaborative work culture. *Educational Leadership, 49*(5), 19-22.

Fullan, M. (1993). Why teachers must become change agents. *Educational Leadership, 50*(6), 12-17.

Fullan, M. (1994). Coordinating top-down and bottom-up strategies for educational reform. *The governance of curriculum: 1994 ASCD Yearbook* (pp. 186-202). Alexandria, VA: ASCD.

Fullan, M. (1995). The school as a learning organization: Distant dreams. *Theory Into Practice, 34,* 230-235.

Fullan, M. (1996). Turning systemic thinking on its head. *Phi Delta Kappan, 77,* 420-423.

Gardner, H. (1983). *Frames of mind: The theory of multiple intelligences.* New York: Basic Books.

Gardner, H. (1991). *The unschooled mind: How children think and how schools should teach.* New York: Basic Books.

Gardner, H., & Boix-Mansilla, V. (1994). Teaching for understanding—within and across disciplines. *Educational Leadership, 51*(5), 14-17.

Garmston, R., Lindner, C., & Whitaker, J. (1993). Reflections on cognitive coaching. *Educational Leadership, 51*(2), 57-61.

Garmston, R., & Wellman, B. (1994). Insights from constructivist learning theory. *Educational Leadership, 51*(7), 84-85.

Gauld, J. (1997, April 23). Why American education is failing. *Education Week, 16,* 41.

Gitlin, A., & Price, K. (1992). Teacher empowerment and the development voice. In C. Glickman (Ed.), *Supervision in transition: 1992 ASCD Yearbook.* Alexandria, VA: ASCD.

Glasser, W. (1990). *The quality school: Managing students without coercion.* New York: Perennial Library.

Glickman, C. (1992). The essence of school renewal: The prose has begun. *Educational Leadership, 50*(1), 24-27.

Glickman, C. (1993). *Renewing America's schools: A guide for school-based action.* San Francisco: Jossey-Bass.

Glickman, C. (1994). Factors affecting school change: For schools participating in the League of Professional Schools. *Journal of Staff Development, 15,* 38-41.

Goertz, M., Floden, R., & O'Day, J. (1996). *Studies of education reform: Vol. 1. Systemic reform.* Washington, DC: U.S. Department of Education, Office of Educational Research and Improvement.

Goldberg, M. (1997). Doing what works: An interview with E. D. Hirsch, Jr. *Phi Delta Kappan, 79,* 83-85.

Good, T., & Brophy, J. (1984). *Looking in classrooms.* New York: Harper & Row.

Good, T., & Brophy, J. (1986). *Educational psychology.* New York: Longman.

Goodlad, J. (1984). *A place called school.* New York: McGraw-Hill.

Gordon, R. (1998). Balancing real-world problems with real-world results. *Phi Delta Kappan, 79,* 390-393.

Gough, P. (1996). Editorial. *Phi Delta Kappan, 77,* 459.

Gregorc, A. (1984). Style as a symptom: A phenomenological perspective. *Theory Into Practice, 23*(1), 51-55.

Grimmett, P. P. (1996). The struggles of teacher research in a context of education reform: Implications for instructional supervision. *Journal of Curriculum and Supervision, 12,* 37-65.

Guilford, J. (1967). *The nature of human intelligence.* New York: McGraw-Hill.

Guskey, T. R. (1994). Making the grade: What benefits students. *Educational Leadership, 52*(2), 14-20.

Guskey, T. R. (1996a). Introduction. In T. R. Guskey (Ed.), *Communicating student learning: 1996 ASCD Yearbook* (pp. 1-5). Alexandria, VA: ASCD.

Guskey, T. R. (1996b). The role of cooperative learning: Lessons from the past—prescriptions for the future. In T. R. Guskey (Ed.), *Communicating student learning: 1996 ASCD Yearbook* (pp. 13-24). Alexandria, VA: ASCD.

Guthrie, J. (1997, October 15). The paradox of educational power. *Education Week, 17,* 34.

Harris, K. R., & Pressley, M. (1991). The nature of cognitive strategy instruction: Interactive strategy construction. *Exceptional Children, 57*(5), 392-403.

Hatch, T. (1998). How comprehensive can comprehensive reform be? *Phi Delta Kappan, 79,* 518-522.

Hawkes, M., & Kimmelman, P. (1997). Go for the goal: First in the world consortium of 20 Chicago-area school districts. *American School Board Journal, 184,* 26-27.

Henry, G., & Sparks, D. (1996). Community accountability: A theory of information, accountability, and school improvement. *Phi Delta Kappan, 78,* 85-90.

Herbert, J. M., & Tankersley, M. (1993). More and less effective ways to intervene with classroom teachers. *Journal of Curriculum and Supervision, 9,* 24-40.

Hersey, P., & Blanchard, K. (1977). *Management of organizational behavior.* Englewood Cliffs, NJ: Prentice Hall.

Hershberg, T. (1997). The case for new standards in education. *Education Week, 17*(16), 52, 32.

Hiebert, J., Carpenter, T., Fennema, E., Fuson, K., Human, P., Murray, H., Olivier, A., & Wearne, D. (1996). Problem-solving as a basis for reform in curriculum and instruction: The case of mathematics. *Educational Leadership, 25*(4), 12-20.

Hirsch, S. (1997, November). *Results,* p. 5.

Hoff, D. (1997a). Latest testing compromise appears doomed. *Education Week, 17*(10), 22.

Hoff, D. (1997b). Measuring Title I's effectiveness. *Education Week, 17*(8), 16-18.

Holcomb, E. (1993). *School-based instructional leadership: A staff development program for school effectiveness and improvement.* Madison, WI: National Center for Effective Schools Research and Development.

Holcomb, E. (1996). *Asking the right questions: Tools and techniques for teamwork.* Thousand Oaks, CA: Corwin.

Holcomb, E., & McCue, L. (1991). *A handbook for implementing school improvement.* Madison, WI: National Center for Effective Schools Research and Development.

Holland, P. E., Clift, R. T., & Veal, M. L. (1992). Linking preservice and inservice supervision through professional inquiry. In C. Glickman (Ed.), *Supervision in transition: 1992 ASCD Yearbook* (pp. 169-182). Alexandria, VA: ASCD.

Honig, B. (1994). How can Horace be helped? *Phi Delta Kappan, 76,* 794.

Hopfenberg, W., & Levin, H. (1993). *The Accelerated Schools resource guide.* San Francisco: Jossey-Bass.

Houston, P. (1994). Don't be bamboozled! Our SAT success story. *Education Digest, 60,* 27-28.

Houston, P. (1997, June 4). Raising the caution flag on the standards movement. *Education Week, 16,* 44.

Hunter, M. (1984). Knowing, teaching, and supervising. In P. Hosford (Ed.), *Using what we know about teaching* (pp. 169-175). Alexandria, VA: ASCD.

Hunter, M. (1988). Create rather than await your fate in teacher evaluation. In S. Stanley & W. J. Popham (Eds.), *Teacher evaluation: Six prescriptions for success* (pp. 32-54). Alexandria, VA: ASCD.

Hunter, M. (1993). Authentic assessment of teaching. *Catalyst for Change, 22,* 5-6.

Hyerle, D. (1996). *Visual tools for construct knowledge.* Alexandria, VA: ASCD.

Jacobs, H. (1989). *Interdisciplinary curriculum: Design and implementation.* Alexandria, VA: ASCD.

Jacobs, H. (1991). Planning for curriculum integration. *Educational Leadership, 49*(2), 27-28.

Jacobs, H. (1997). *Mapping the big picture.* Alexandria, VA: ASCD.

Jennings, J. (1997, November 26). Opportunity to learn or opportunity to lose? *Education Week, 17*(14), 44, 32.

Jervis, K., & McDonald, J. (1996). Standards: The philosophical monster in the classroom. *Phi Delta Kappan, 77,* 563-569.

Joyce, B., & Showers, B. (1996). The evolution of peer coaching. *Educational Leadership, 53*(6), 12-16.

Kane, M., & Khattri, N. (1995). Assessment reform: A work in progress. *Phi Delta Kappan, 77,* 30-32.

Kearns, D., & Doyle, D. (1988). *Winning the brain race.* San Francisco: ICS.

Keller, B. (1995). Accelerated Schools: Hands-on learning in a unified community. *Educational Leadership, 52*(5), 10-13.

Killion, J., & Hirsch, S. (1998). A crack in the middle: Staff development for middle school teachers. *Education Week, 17*(27), 44.

Klein, S., Medrich, E., & Perez-Ferreiro, V. (1996). Fitting the pieces: Education reform that works. In *OERI studies of education reform.* Washington, DC: U.S. Department of Education.

Klitgaard, G. (1987). The principal's role in helping teachers manage their classrooms. *National Association of Secondary School Principals Bulletin, 71*(502), 64-67.

Koba, S. (1996). Narrowing the achievement gap in science: Implementing an integrated science curriculum in Omaha, Nebraska. *Educational Leadership, 53,* 14-17.

Kohn, A. (1994). Grading: The issue is not how but why. *Educational Leadership, 52*(2), 38-41.

Kohn, A. (1996). What to look for in a classroom. *Educational Leadership, 54*(1), 54-55.

Krumboltz, J., & Yeh, C. (1996). Competitive grading sabotages good teaching. *Phi Delta Kappan, 78,* 324-326.

Lamb, R., & Thomas, M. (1981). The art and science of teacher evaluation. *Principal, 61*(1), 44-47.

Lawton, M. (1996). Math, science curricula said to fall short. *Education Week, 16*(7), 1, 9.

Lawton, M. (1998a). Evolution debate accents deeper science disquiet. *Education Week, 17*(34), 1, 17.

Lawton, M. (1998b). Reporter's notebook. *Education Week, 17*(33), 14.

Levine, D., & Lezotte, L. (1990). *Unusually effective schools: A review and analysis of research and practice.* Madison, WI: National Center for Effective Schools Research and Development.

Lewis, A. (1997). The price of poverty. *Phi Delta Kappan, 78,* 423-424.

Lewis, A. (1998). School-to-work, certificate of mastery, and standards. *Phi Delta Kappan, 79,* 563-564.

Lezotte, L. (1994). The nexus of instructional leadership and effective schools. *School Administrator, 51,* 20-22.

Lieberman, A. (1991). Accountability as a reform strategy. *Phi Delta Kappan, 73,* 219-220.

Lofland, G. (1995). Where children come first. *Educational Leadership, 52*(5), 16-18.

Loveless, T. (1997). The second great math rebellion. *Education Week, 17*(7), 48, 36.

Maeroff, G. (1993). Building teams to rebuild schools. *Phi Delta Kappan, 74,* 512-519.

Manatt, R. (1987). Lesson from a comprehensive performance appraisal project. *Educational Leadership, 44*(7), 8-14.

Manatt, R. (1988). Teacher performance evaluation: A total systems approach. In S. Stanley & W. J. Popham (Eds.), *Teacher evaluation: Six prescriptions for success* (pp. 79-108). Alexandria, VA: ASCD.

Manatt, R., Palmer, K., & Hidlebaugh, E. (1976). Evaluating teacher performance with improved rating scales. *National Association of Secondary School Principals Bulletin, 60*(401), 21-24.

March, J., Peters, K., & Adler, H. (1994). Peer coaching: Empowering teachers while accomplishing management goals. *Government Union Review, 15*(2), 44-62.

Marzano, R., Pickering, D., & McTighe, J. (1992). *Dimensions of learning: Teaching with a different kind of classroom.* Alexandria, VA: ASCD.

Marzano, R., Pickering, D., & McTighe, J. (1993). *Assessing student outcomes: Performance assessment using the dimensions of learning model.* Alexandria, VA: ASCD.

McAdams, R. (1997). A systems approach to school reform. *Phi Delta Kappan, 79,* 138-142.

McCarthy, B. (1990). Using the 4MAT system to bring learning styles to schools. *Educational Leadership, 48*(2), 31-37.

McGreal, T. (1988). Evaluation for enhancing instruction: Linking teacher evaluation and staff development. In S. Stanley & W. J. Popham (Eds.), *Teacher evaluation: Six prescriptions for success* (pp. 1-29). Alexandria, VA: ASCD.

McLaughlin, M., & Talbert, J. (1994). Teacher professionalism in local school contexts. *American Journal of Education, 102,* 123-153.

Meier, D. (1995). How our schools could be. *Phi Delta Kappan, 76,* 369-373.

Meier, D. (1998). Regarding portfolios: Peter Berger's critique of portfolios [Letter to the editor]. *Education Week, 17*(23), 40.

Metzger, M. (1996). Maintaining a life. *Phi Delta Kappan, 77,* 347-351.

Mizell, H. (1997, November). *Results,* p. 5.

Murnane, R., & Levy, F. (1996a). Sizing up market-based education reforms. *Education Digest, 62,* 10-14.

Murnane, R., & Levy, F. (1996b, September 11). Why money matters sometimes. *Education Week, 16*(2), 48, 36-37.

National Association of Elementary Principals. (1988). *Effective teacher: Effective evaluation.* Alexandria, VA: Author.

National Commission on Testing and Public Policy. (1991). *From gatekeeper to gateway: Transforming testing in America.* Chestnut Hill, MA: Author.

Newmann, F. M. (1996). *Linking restructuring to authentic student achievement: A handbook for student performance assessment.* Alexandria, VA: ASCD.

Nolan, J., Francis, P., & Hawkes, B. (1993). Case studies: Windows onto clinical supervision. *Educational Leadership, 51*(2), 52-56.

Odden, A., & Wohlstetter, P. (1995). Making school-based management work. *Educational Leadership, 52*(5), 32-36.

Olson, L. (1997). Quality counts. *Education Week, 17*(15), 5.

O'Neil, J. (1995). On lasting school reform: A conversation with Ted Sizer. *Educational Leadership, 52*(5), 4-9.

Pace-Marshall, S., & Hatcher, C. (1996). Promoting career development through CADRE. *Educational Leadership, 53*(6), 42-46.

Pallrand, G. (1996). The relationship of assessment to knowledge development in science education. *Phi Delta Kappan, 78,* 315-318.

Palmer, J. M. (1995). Interdisciplinary curriculum—again. In J. A. Beane (Ed.), *Toward a coherent curriculum: 1995 ASCD Yearbook* (pp. 55-61). Alexandria, VA: ASCD.

Parish, R., & Aquila, F. (1996). Cultural ways of working and believing in school: Preserving the way things are. *Phi Delta Kappan, 78*, 298-305.

Pate, E., McGinnis, K., & Homestead, E. (1995). Creating coherence through curriculum integration. In J. A. Beane (Ed.), *Toward a coherent curriculum: 1995 ASCD Yearbook* (pp. 62-70). Alexandria, VA: ASCD.

Peel, J., & McCary, C. E. (1997). Visioning the "little red schoolhouse" for the 21st century. *Phi Delta Kappan, 78*, 698-699.

Perkins, D. (1992). *Smart schools: From training memories to educating minds.* New York: Free Press.

Perkins, D., & Saloman, G. (1989). Are cognitive skills context-bound? *Educational Researcher, 8*(1), 16-25.

Perrone, V. (1991). *A letter to teachers: Reflections on schooling and the art of teaching.* San Francisco: Jossey-Bass.

Perrone, V. (1994). How to engage students in learning. *Educational Leadership, 51*(5), 11-13.

Piaget, J. (1952). *The origins of intelligence in children.* New York: International University Press.

Piaget, J. (1966). *The child's conception of physical causality.* London: Routledge & Kegan Paul.

Piaget, J. (1970). Piaget's theory. In P. Mussen (Ed.), *Carmichael's manual of child psychology.* New York: John Wiley.

Pintrich, P. (1993). Beyond cold conceptual change: The role of motivational beliefs and classroom contextual factors in the process of conceptual change. *Review of Educational Research, 63*(2), 67-99.

Pipho, C. (1996). Stateline. *Phi Delta Kappan, 77*, 463.

Pipho, C. (1998). The value added side of standards. *Phi Delta Kappan, 79*, 341-342.

Pogrow, S. (1996). Reforming the wannabe reformers: Why educational reform almost always ends up making things worse. *Phi Delta Kappan, 77*, 656-663.

Pogrow, S. (1997). The tyranny and folly of ideological progressivism. *Education Week, 17*(12), 34, 36.

Ponessa, J. (1996). Chain of blame: When a student shows up for college unprepared to do the work, who is responsible? *Education Week, 15*(35), 29-33.

Poole, W. (1994). Removing "super" from supervision. *Journal of Curriculum and Supervision, 9*, 284-309.

Popham, W. J. (1998). Farewell, curriculum: Confessions of an assessment convert. *Phi Delta Kappan, 79*, 380-384.

Prince, J. (1983-1984). Formative teacher evaluation: The crucial element in an outcome-based education program. In K. Klein (Ed.), *Evaluation of teaching: The formative process* (pp. 85-94). Bloomington, IN: Phi Delta Kappa Educational Foundation, Center on Evaluation, Development, and Research.

Ramirez-Smith, C. (1995). Stopping the cycle of failure: The Comer model. *Educational Leadership, 52*(5), 14-18.

Ravitch, D. (1992, April). *Federal reform in education: Boon or bane?* Paper presented at the annual meeting of the American Educational Research Association, San Francisco.

Reigeluth, C. (1997a). Educational standards: To standardize or to customize learning? *Phi Delta Kappan, 79*, 202-206.

Reigeluth, C. (1997b). Instructional theory, practitioner needs, and new directions: Some reflections. *Educational Technology, 37*, 42-47.

Renyi, J. (1996). The longest reform: When teachers take charge of their own learning. *Education Week, 16*(11), 34, 37.

Renyi, J. (1998). Building learning into the teaching job. *Educational Leadership, 55*(5), 70-74.

Resnick, L. B. (1987). *Education and learning to think.* Washington, DC: Academic Press.

Resnick, L. (1994). Situating rationalism: Biological and social preparation for learning. In L. Hirschfeld & S. Gelmann (Eds.), *Mapping the mind: Domain specificity in cognition and culture* (pp. 474-494). Cambridge: Cambridge University Press.

Rich, D. (1997, August 6). Seven habits of good teachers today. *Education Week, 16*, 53.

Rose, L., Elam, S., & Gallup, A. (1995). The 27th annual Phi Delta Kappa/Gallup poll of the public's attitudes toward the public schools. *Phi Delta Kappan, 77*, 41-56.

Rose, L., Elam, S., & Gallup, A. (1996). The 28th annual Phi Delta Kappa/Gallup poll of the public's attitudes toward the public schools. *Phi Delta Kappan, 78*, 41-59.

Rose, L., Elam, S., & Gallup, A. (1997). The 29th annual Phi Delta Kappa/Gallup poll of the public's attitudes toward the public schools. *Phi Delta Kappan, 79*, 42-56.

Rosenshine, B. (1983). Teaching functions in instructional programs. *Elementary School Journal, 83,* 335-351.

Rossi, R., & Stringfield, S. (1995). What we must do for students placed at risk. *Phi Delta Kappan, 77,* 73-76.

Rotberg, I., Futrell, M., & Lieberman, J. (1998). National board certification: Increasing participation and assessing impacts. *Phi Delta Kappan, 79,* 462-466.

Rothman, R. (1996). Linking standards and instruction—HELPS is on the way. *Educational Leadership, 53*(8), 44-46.

Rothman, R. (1997). KERA: A tale of one school. *Phi Delta Kappan, 79,* 272-275.

Rowley, J., & Hart, P. (1996). How video case studies can promote reflective dialogue. *Educational Leadership, 53*(6), 28-29.

Sadler, N. (1982). The appraisal interview: Management techniques for evaluating teachers. *National Association of Secondary School Principals Bulletin, 66*(458), 1-8.

Sahakian, P., & Stockton, J. (1996). Opening doors: Teacher-guided observation. *Educational Leadership, 53*(6), 50-53.

Sarason, S. (1990). *The predictable failure of school reform.* San Francisco: Jossey-Bass.

Sarason, S. (1993a). *The case for change: Rethinking the preparation of educators.* San Francisco: Jossey-Bass.

Sarason, S. (1993b). *Letters to a serious education president.* Newbury Park, CA: Corwin.

Sarason, S. (1995). Some reaction to what we have learned. *Phi Delta Kappan, 77,* 84-85.

Schlechty, P. (1990). *Schools for the 21st century: Leadership imperatives for educational reform.* San Francisco: Jossey-Bass.

Schlechty, P. (1994). *Increasing student engagement.* Missouri Leadership Academy.

Schuster, E. (1998). Our tests, ourselves. *Education Week, 17*(30), 34.

Searfoss, L. W., & Enz, B. J. (1996). Can teacher evaluation reflect holistic instruction? *Educational Leadership, 53*(6), 38-41.

Secretary's Commission on Achieving Necessary Skills. (1991). *What work requires of schools: A SCANS report for America 2000.* Washington, DC: Author.

Seeley, D. (1998, January 21). The best (only?) alternative to vouchers. *Education Week, 17,* 60.

Semb, G., & Ellis, J. (1994). Knowledge taught in school: What is remembered? *Review of Educational Research, 64,* 253-286.

Senge, P. (1990). *The fifth discipline: The art and practice of the learning organization.* New York: Doubleday/Currency.

Senge, P. (1997a). Foreword. In A. L. Costa & R. M. Liebmann (Eds.), *Envisioning process as content: Toward a renaissance curriculum* (pp. vii-xii). Thousand Oaks, CA: Corwin.

Senge, P. (1997b). Foreword. In A. L. Costa & R. M. Liebmann (Eds.), *The process-centered school: Sustaining a renaissance community* (pp. vii-xii). Thousand Oaks, CA: Corwin.

Shanker, A. (1990). Staff development and the restructured school. *1990 ASCD Yearbook* (pp. 91-103). Alexandria, VA: ASCD.

Shanker, A. (1995). A reflection on 12 studies of education reform. *Phi Delta Kappan, 77,* 81-82.

Shavelson, R. (1997, May 7). The splintered curriculum. *Education Week, 16,* 38.

Shepard, L. (1989). Why we need better assessments. *Educational Leadership, 46*(7), 4-9.

Shepard, L. (1993). *Lifting the veil: The feminine face of science.* Boston: Shambhala.

Shepard, L. (1995). Using assessment to improve learning. *Educational Leadership, 52*(5), 38-43.

Shields, P., & Knapp, M. (1997). The promise and limits of school-based reform: A national snapshot. *Phi Delta Kappan, 79,* 288-294.

Sizer, T. (1992a, April). *Federal reform in education: Boon or bane?* Paper presented at the annual meeting of the American Educational Research Association, San Francisco.

Sizer, T. (1992b). *Horace's school: Redesigning the American high school.* Boston: Houghton Mifflin.

Slavin, R., Madden, N., & Karweit, N. (1990). Success for all: First-year outcomes of a comprehensive plan for reforming urban education. *American Educational Research Journal, 27,* 255-278.

Snow, R. (1997). Aptitudes and symbol systems in adaptive classroom teaching. *Phi Delta Kappan, 78,* 354-360.

Sousa, D. (1992). Helping students remember what you teach. *Middle School Journal, 23*(5), 21-23.

Spady, W. G. (1994). Choosing outcomes of significance. *Educational Leadership, 51*(6), 18-22.

Sparks, D. (1997a, November). Editorial. *Results,* p. 5.

Sparks, D. (1997b). An interview with Linda Darling-Hammond. *Tour of Staff Development, 18*(1), 34-35.

Stake, R. (1991). The teacher, standardized testing, and prospects of revolution. *Phi Delta Kappan, 73,* 243-247.

Sternberg, R. (1990). Thinking styles: Keys to understanding student performance. *Phi Delta Kappan, 71,* 366-371.

Sternberg, R. (1997, December 3). A waste of talent. *Education Week, 17*(15), 56.

Stiggins, R. J. (1994). Keeping performance assessment in perspective. *Student centered classroom assessment.* New York: Macmillan.

Stiggins, R. J., & Conklin, N. F. (1992). *In teachers' hands: Investigating the practices of classroom assessment.* Albany: SUNY Press.

Stigler, J., & Hiebert, J. (1997). Understanding and improving class mathematics instruction: An overview of the TIMSS video study. *Phi Delta Kappan, 79,* 14-21.

Stow, S., & Sweeney, J. (1981). Developing a teacher performance evaluation system. *Educational Leadership, 38*(7), 538-541.

Strong, R., Silver, F., & Robinson, A. (1995). What do students want—and what really motivates them? *Educational Leadership, 53*(1), 8-12.

Sweeney, J. (1982). Planning makes a difference: Improving the post-observation conference. *National Association of Secondary School Principals Bulletin, 66*(458), 38-40.

Sylwester, R. (1995). *A celebration of neurons: An educator's guide to the human brain.* Alexandria, VA: ASCD.

Taba, H. (1966). *Teaching strategies and cognitive functioning in elementary school children.* San Francisco Cooperative Research Project #2404—State College, San Francisco.

Taylor, B. (1984). *Implementing what works: Elementary principals and school improvement programs* (Doctoral dissertation, Northwestern University, 1984; University Microfilms International #8502445).

Taylor, B., & Bullard, P. (1994). *Keepers of the dream: The triumph of effective schools.* Chicago: Excelsior!

Taylor, B., & Bullard, P. (1995). *The revolution revisited: Effective schools and systemic reform.* Bloomington, IN: Phi Delta Kappa Educational Foundation.

Taylor, B., & Levine, D. (1991). Effective schools projects and school-based management. *Phi Delta Kappan, 72,* 394-397.

Taylor, B., & Walton, S. (1997). Co-opting standardized tests in the service of learning. *Phi Delta Kappan, 79,* 66-70.

Terwilliger, J. (1997). Semantics, psychometrics, and assessment reform: A close look at "authentic" assessments. *Educational Researcher, 26,* 24-27.

Thorpe, R. (1997). The "still, small voice" of reform. *Education Week, 17*(5), 34, 38.

Tishman, S., & Perkins, D. (1997). The language of thinking. *Phi Delta Kappan, 78,* 368-374.

Tucker, M., & Codding, J. (1998). *Standards for our schools: How to set them, measure them, and reach them.* San Francisco: Jossey-Bass.

Tyack, D., & Cuban, L. (1995). *Tinkering toward utopia: A century of public school reform.* Cambridge, MA: Harvard University Press.

Tyler, R. W. (1950). *Basic principles of curriculum and instruction.* Chicago: University of Chicago Press.

Viadero, D. (1997, November 12). Accrediting bodies offer improvement guide. *Education Week, 17,* 5.

Vygotsky, L. (1936). *Thought and language.* Cambridge: MIT Press.

Wagner, T. (1994). *How schools change: Lessons from 3 communities.* Boston, MA: Beacon Press.

Wagner, T. (1998, April 22). From compliance to collaboration: Four leadership qualities needed to change schools. *Education Week, 17*(32), 36, 40.

Watts, K. H. (1996). Bridges freeze before roads. In T. R. Guskey (Ed.), *Communicating student learning: 1996 ASCD Yearbook* (pp. 6-12). Alexandria, VA: ASCD.

Wheatley, M. (1992). *Leadership and the new science.* San Francisco: Berrett Koehler.

Whimbey, A. (1995). *Analytical reading and reasoning.* Cary, NC: Innovative.

Wiggins, G. (1992). Creating tests worth taking. *Educational Leadership, 49*(8), 26-33.

Wiggins, G. (1993). *Assessing student performance: Exploring the purpose and limits of testing.* San Francisco: Jossey-Bass.

Wiggins, G. (1995a). Curricular coherence and assessment: Making sure that the effect matches the intent. In J. A. Beane (Ed.), *Toward a coherent curriculum: 1995 ASCD Yearbook* (pp. 101-119). Alexandria, VA: ASCD.

Wiggins, G. (1995b). Standards, not standardization: Evoking quality student work. In A. Ornstein & L. Behar (Eds.), *Contemporary issues in curriculum* (pp. 187-195). Boston: Allyn & Bacon.

Wiggins, G. (1996). Embracing accountability. *New Schools, New Communities, 12*(2), 4-10.

Winner, E. (1996). The miseducation of our gifted children. *Education Week, 16*(7), 44,35.

Wise, A. E., & Leibrand, J. (1996). Profession-based accreditation: A foundation for high-quality teaching. *Phi Delta Kappan, 78,* 202-206.

Wlodkowski, R., & Ginsberg, M. (1995). A framework for culturally responsive teaching. *Educational Leadership, 53*(1), 17-21.

Wohlstetter, P. (1995). Getting school-based management right: What works and what doesn't? *Phi Delta Kappan, 77,* 22-26.

Zemelman, S., Daniels, H., & Hyde, A. (1993). *Best practice: New standards for teaching and learning in America's schools.* Portsmouth, NH: Heinemann.

INDEX